The
Recharged
Woman

Success Strategies for Energizing Your Life

Pam Potter Nelson

Andover, MN

[handwritten inscription:] Connie — Cong[ratulations] becoming

[handwritten:] Here's to sitting on the curb!

[handwritten signature:] Recharged, Pam Nelson

Author photo by Elusive Image Photography.

ISBN 1-931945-09-8

Library of Congress Catalog Number: 2003112783

Printed in the United States

First Printing: November 2003

07 06 05 04 03   6 5 4 3 2 1

Expert Publishing, Inc.
14314 Thrush Street NW, Andover, MN 55304-3330
1-877-755-4966
www.ExpertPublishingInc.com

Table of Contents

Acknowledgement

Acknowledgement

If you believe that people are brought into our lives for a reason, then Harry and Sharron Stockhausen are proof positive. Sharron (Stockhausen Ink) edited with professional detail and never used the intimidating red pen to point out errors. Her perseverance in holding me accountable for a quality product was tempered by her encouraging words and warm hugs, her endless humor, and her insightful suggestions when I hit a creative wall.

Harry's teddy-bear demeanor made it easy for me to commit to this humbling endeavor. His broad-based knowledge and negotiating expertise in the publications industry left me confident that the details would be handled flawlessly. Expert Publishing, Inc. has served me well.

Friend and speaking colleague, Janna Krammer, convinced me to transform my thoughts onto paper. She coached me to discover the book's main title, *The Recharged Woman*. Janna is a special gift in my life.

I am eternally grateful to my parents, William and Valorie Potter, who modeled realistic values and held my sister and me responsible for living life with those values. They raised us to ask questions and take our potential to the next level. I appreciate their commitment to challenge us to develop our own unique identities and define success from our own perspective. They instilled in each of us the spirit behind the Recharged Woman. Both of them believe that anything is possible with the right attitude. They have continued to remind me of that fact throughout this whole writing process.

I'm not certain that my husband, Steve, always knew what direction I was taking with this book, but he certainly gave me the space to pursue my goal. Without his loving, but direct reminders to manage the many piles of papers, I might have given up long ago on this valuable resource tool for women. I appreciate his efforts to make time for play together (especially on the golf course and mountain ski runs), nurture our marriage, and help with the dishes after late-evening meals.

Ah, Erik, not only has it been a privilege to be your parent and confidant, but also it's been a joy to see you grow in so many ways. As a high school student, you agreed to utilize your own personal coach. You inspired other teens to get in touch with something deeper than the social and academic demands of school. As an only child, you paid the price of living in an adult world, and at the same time reaped the benefits of living in an adult world. You traveled as far away as Australia and rubbed elbows with VIPs all over the world. Yet, you learned to appreciate the solitude of sitting in a duck blind and tending to a cozy fire in the middle of the woods. At the young age of twenty, you found your passion and declared that you were charging forward to create a life in that direction. What an inspiration you are to so many of my friends, seminar audiences, and coaching clients, many of whom at age forty plus are trying to realize and pursue their passion. What a learning experience it is for me to see the process in action. Thanks for turning the tables on me and coaching me around life balance. Your invitation (insistence) to ski Big Sky recharged a part of me I'd left behind when we as a family committed to support your love of ice hockey. Thanks for including me among your friends.

Without my sister's creative talents, I would be without a subtitle and chapter titles. More than a sister, Lynn Potter-Goldstein, you model personal balance like no other business owner I know (Paradise Adventure Group and Oz Dive). You are so tuned into your boundaries, live life from your clearly defined set of values, nurture the relationships that matter, clean your life of clutter, and enjoy life with such freedom and peace. I am honored to know you. Plainly put, you are who women strive to be. You are the epitome of the Recharged Woman.

Your thought-provoking questions, Jay Goldstein, always took me to a deeper level of emotional, thoughtful, and spiritual learning. Your subtle guidance in the development of this book is noted. Thanks for bringing laughter to my life. I deeply value your friendship.

Dr. Gloria Goldstein, founder of Polish Your Potential, was instrumental in coaching me toward this point in time. You are a trusted friend and motivator. Coachy Coachy, everyone in the Houston, Texas, area should be using your consulting and coaching services.

Reverend Ryan Alexander created a safe space for me to begin to learn to speak and write about God openly. I am still learning every day to appreciate His blessings.

Heather Fine of Elusive Image Photography and Laura Warrick of L Warrick Photography, thanks for capturing the better side of me.

I am grateful to the many business acquaintances, friends, coaching clients, and speaking and seminar associates whose input have been invaluable. In particular I'd like to mention Michelle Neujahr, for her ability to tell stories (although she has yet to teach me the principles behind compelling story telling), and Barry ZeVan, former television news personality, for providing business contacts and helping promote the book.

Thank you to everyone across the world who fearlessly accepts a coaching challenge, whether you are a client or not. Isn't it exciting to have an ah-hah experience that takes you to a new level of discovery, choice, and ultimately to lasting change? If even for a moment, isn't it exhilarating to recharge? And to think, you can have it every day.

Dedication

Dedication

This book is dedicated to my maternal Grandma Lil who courageously battled breast cancer from the perspective of living life passionately, with grace and dignity; whose gifts of hope, unconditional love, and dedication to her faith in Jesus Christ were gleaned from that special place on her lap in her rocking chair. (Grandma, you'd be tickled pink to know that your great grandson spent countless hours in that same rocking chair on many a special lap.)

I also dedicate this book to my mother, mom, best friend, and confidant, Val, for emulating all that is good in life, much of what she learned from her mother. She is the lightning rod to grounding me in reality. She taught me everything I share with others in this book, and more. She also taught me that women can have brass balls, soft hearts, and be respected and appreciated for both. Before there was such a buzzword, Mom showed me how to "balance" life through non-negotiable values, self love (and love for others), passion and the desire to follow it, faith, intuition, forthright commitment, humor (especially in times of adversity), and a shamelessly positive attitude. She is the epitome of the Recharged Woman. Thanks, Mom, "I am" because of you. I love you more than words can express.

Introduction

Introduction

I am the reason I wrote this book. You are the reason I wrote this book. Our lives are complicated. For most of us, it seems there is seldom time to do what we truly find enjoyable. We are caught up in the chaos of unplanned events, emergencies, the needs of others, job security, social and family obligations, and more.

Hey, let's face it. At some point as we matured, each of us grabbed life by the tail. For the most part, it was good. At each stepping stone we thought we knew it all. We thought we had it all. Then, as the clutter set in, our expectations for a dream life ran into the wall of reality. Our vision turned foggy. The lights dimmed. For some of us, the lights went out.

Are you overwhelmed with the vast responsibilities that encompass your days, weeks, and months? Where has your year gone? The last three years? Does the minute hand on your clock seem to tick faster than everyone else's? Is there more mental and emotional fatigue than healthy physical fatigue in your pattern of living? Do you feel consumed by the stressors in your life? Do they appear to control your activities, leaving little if any time for you? Does guilt land on your shoulder every time you consider taking care of yourself? Are you unplugged from your basic needs? Do you even recognize the "disconnect" any more? Do the words "Stop. Breathe." ring a bell?

What would life be like if all your negative, self limiting "what if's" were replaced by the "what if's" of your potential? What if you could clearly see where the interconnectedness of the various parts of your life was short-circuited? What if you could reconnect those parts into a more balanced scenario for a truly satisfying life?

What if your life was less stressful? What if your bad habits were replaced with new habits that strengthened your chance for success? What if you could define your own success? What if you could embrace and implement new skills that increased your happiness and personal satisfaction with life? What if a bit of the leader in you was revealed in such a way that you took back control of the life you lost to circumstance? What if you could increase your personal self-awareness, replenish your energy, and live the life you yearn to reclaim? What if you could accomplish it without having to read a book from cover to cover?

Well, you can have it all and more. What's more, life can be satisfying and fulfilling today and long into the future.

You and I were once charged with energy, enthusiasm, and spirit. Stuff got in the way, and after a while we stopped noticing the missing links to staying charged. We desperately sought change, yet we didn't quite know how to implement it.

The Recharged Woman creates a framework of conduits (tools) for your personal use. It explores simple, real-life success strategies for regaining the physical, emotional, and spiritual gifts that are buried deep inside you. It does so from a no-nonsense, bottom-line approach void of the flowery woo-woo of so many self-help books. As you begin to identify the Recharged Woman from within, you will discover what's not working, make responsible, meaningful choices around diminishing the current chaotic, exhausting lifestyle, commit to meaningful change, and invest in one or more action steps to take control internally as well as externally.

You'll explore your values and attitudes, lock in your ardent purpose and begin to regain the balance that delights you and those around you. You'll create much-needed boundaries, experience contentment while moving forward in life. You'll strategize relationship building and decide what really matters. As you engage in recharging yourself, so will you naturally recharge others.

Your self-esteem, identity, and confidence will become clearer as you strengthen your listening and requesting skills. You'll develop the basic coaching skills that Recharged Women all over the world embrace every day. Who said you couldn't afford to have your own coach in a pocket? I challenge you to plug in, power up, and switch on! You are about to celebrate *being* the Recharged Woman!

Main $\mathscr{Switches}$

We need the basics of oxygen to breathe, food to sustain our physical and nutritional health, and robust organs to keep our body functioning and physically energized. Much like these physical needs, Main Switches are our mental, spiritual, and emotional electrifiers. They are the building blocks that replenish our energy and allow us to recharge.

First Things First—
Achieving *Awareness*

She looks in the mirror, knowing society labels her successful. She is educated, owns a beautifully appointed home, maintains a 25-plus year loving relationship with her husband, works hard, plays harder, and enjoys many of the material comforts of life. She owns cars and antique jars, and celebrates holidays afar. She peddles a bicycle, straddles a noisy motorcycle, and runs on an elliptical exercise machine she calls, "Michael." She possesses golf clubs, swirling bathtubs, and gourmet meat spices called rubs. Outwardly, she plays the success game quite well. Her intellectual knowledge and material lifestyle, however, leave her with a deep, empty chasm on the inside. It's true; she is never really settled or happy. There is no contentment or tranquility. She is driven to look for what's next without taking time to appreciate the present.

> *Awareness—you can be only when you can see.*
> —Pamela Nelson

Who is this person behind the façade? Oh my goodness, it's ME!

Caught up in societal expectations, my awareness of the real me from the inside out became a clouded mystery. Somewhere I misplaced much of what I'd learned about being authentic and credible.

Like an instantaneous bolt of lightning searing the night sky, life screamed past me at record speeds. As a wife, hockey mom and caregiver, a business owner, speaker, educator, volunteer, and lifelong learner (what was I really learning anyway?), my roles became blurred. I seemed to feed life's external fires while extinguishing my own. I had forgotten the most important definition of success—inner peace, joy, and fulfillment. I short-circuited and, in the chaos of an action-packed life, I failed to realize the negative impact I was having on myself and those around me

I thought I lived by my values. I believed in my religious upbringing and expressed it routinely. I thought my direction in life was clear, and I knew I would kick my own aspirations into high gear when my son was grown. I thought I was conscientious, goal-driven, and able to say "no" occasionally. I *thought*—

I *thought* I had life figured out, yet I was calculating life instead of thriving "in" my life. I was going with the flow and moving through the motions without connecting to the essence of my feelings and emotions. Simply stated, I lacked a fuller personal self-awareness.

Self-awareness is the process of uncovering the real person inside each of us. It's connecting with our feelings, wisdom, intuition, and peace of mind. Until we discover and become increasingly aware of what short-circuits us, it's impossible to fully appreciate, celebrate, and become the Recharged Woman. When we begin to troubleshoot the short circuits in our life and disconnect them, we can connect to the power circuits that deliver the energy necessary to recharge every day for the rest of our lives.

You've heard the phrase "you don't know what you don't know." I use the phrase "awareness is the seeing and being from the inside out." Are you just going through the motions? Are you hiding from the authentic and unique you, like I did for so many years? Are you possibly confusing the term "success" with external worth and material goods and activities? Do you ever feel like you're missing a deeper meaning in life? Is there more anxiety, disappointment, anger, stress, and emptiness in your life than there is freedom, peace, contentment, and fulfillment?

Conscious awareness awakens the bare-naked truth.
—Pamela Nelson

For me, life's mantra was go with the flow. I just figured every day was a stream of fireworks exploding in all directions. Then my personal coach opened my eyes to a different perspective. Masterfully coached, I uncovered a new level of truth and bare-naked awareness. A bit fearful of exposing what I had hidden for so long (that I didn't realize I was hiding), my curiosity finally got the best of me. I decided to trust the awareness process uncondi- tionally. What did I have to lose? I soon discovered the magnificence of the internal "being" I really am. Oh sure, this inner being has been there all along, and has surfaced on many occasions, but she was slippery and disappeared all too often in the muck of life.

As we journey through the following chapters and engage conscious awareness, we will develop the foun- dational building blocks that illumi- nate our path forward, we will question the short circuits that stop us in our tracks, and we will choose to implement lasting change from the list of electrifying rechargers pre- sented throughout the book. This process guarantees to make life more fulfilling and successful for each of us.

> *Awareness*
> *is the seeing and being*
> *from the inside out.*
> —Pamela Nelson

Exercise—Notice What You Notice

Choose an amount of time, one minute, five minutes, or ten minutes. Turn up your senses 200%. Feel everything that crosses your fingertips. Smell everything around you. Sit in a quiet spot. Listen to your breath. Feel your heartbeat. Smell your skin. Notice how your surround- ings affect you including the temperature of the room, the comfort of the floor, bed, chair, or wherever you are perched. Notice the comfort and discomfort of the moment.

Increase awareness by journaling or tape recording all that you notice. Keep in mind the intensity of this focus exercise as you move forward to a more aware life.

Here are a few questions I use with my coaching clients to begin their personal awareness.

- Amidst the stress and chaos of everyday live, who have I become?
- Where is my attention and focus?
- How does it feel to know I can have a richer, more fulfilling life just by being more aware of who I am?
- What one thing do I choose to engage in today to become more aware of who I am and how I behave?
- What has awareness awakened in me?

The Recharged *Woman*

- The Recharged Woman defines awareness as "the seeing and being from the inside out."
- The Recharged Woman is consciously aware of both her words and feelings as they relate to her growing self-awareness.
- The Recharged Woman trusts her ability to explore the depths of her authentic self through conscious awareness.
- The Recharged Woman knows that insight and understanding are products of conscious awareness. Awareness intensifies over time and brings unlimited freedom to explore her full potential.
- The Recharged Woman defines success as inner peace, joy, and fulfillment.

Attitude is a Voltage Meter

Attitude. You have one! So, do I. Our attitudes are basically positive or negative. It's a matter of choice. It's your choice. It's that simple. It's as simple as toggling the light switch on or off—a positive or negative charge, a positive or negative attitude.

What, then, makes it so incredibly difficult to embrace a positive attitude all the time? Let's face it. Life is filled with the daily flux of commitments and unexpected surprises. Our calendars explode with myriad activities. Some of those activities serve our needs. Most seem to serve our loved ones, society, and work. Chaos, stress, and overwhelming expectations creep into our daily activities almost as silently as static electricity builds into a jolting charge.

> *A strong positive mental attitude will create more miracles than any wonder drug.*
> —Patricia Neal

Life no longer seems to belong to us. We buckle under pressure and often follow the path of least resistance. We feel a loss of control like being sucked into the vortex of a tornado or, better yet, being swirled around and flushed down the toilet of life. That path of least resistance is the negative charge, the dismal attitude where we no longer choose to take full responsibility for our actions and thoughts, that sort of "victim" place. While this place may not meet our physical comforts, victim status is an emotional choice releasing us from decision-making and accountability for outcomes and resulting consequences. It's the place where the blame game is played.

A woman with a discharged power pack allows herself (actually chooses) to be a victim of circumstance and remain attitudinally oppressed. Life bubbles over with fear, anger, self-pity, and loneliness. Anxiety, worry, and pessimism abound. She is suspicious of others' intentions to help her. Life from her perspective "is what it is." This narrow view eliminates all perceived possibility for change. A victim chooses to refuse to take responsibility for her thoughts and actions. The discharged woman chooses to avoid building a critical foundational tool: a positive attitude.

Perhaps you are, by nature, a truly positive person, but shut down from time to time with overwhelming stress and chaos. You're not alone. The mind is powerful. Hmm-m-m. If you're starting to mull over all the activities in your life over which you have no control, congratulations!

Your connecting to self-awareness is a first step to engaging a positive attitude.

We choose to be victims of circumstance just as we choose to stand empowered and victimless. It's a choice of attitudes. And while we cannot control all of life's unknowns, what we can control is our mind's awareness, our attitude, and our response to all that goes on around us. It is YOU and all that happens inwardly with who you are, with who you choose to be, that determines your course of life now and in the future.

We *are* what we *believe*. Thoughts and attitudes go hand in hand. Recurring thoughts mature into attitudes. Attitudes affect present and future life. Destructive attitudes are akin to the demolition team. Negative attitudes discharge. Constructive thoughts and attitudes are brick and mortar, the studs and beams that make way for the finished structure. Positive attitudes energize and recharge.

Lou Holtz is quoted as saying, "Ability is what you're capable of doing. Motivation determines what you do. Attitude determines how well you do it." For months, I thought I could not write this book. I felt stuck and unable to release onto paper the words I had spoken for years. I believed I was not a writer, even though past evidence of writing curriculum, training manuals, and magazine articles proved contrary to the head game I was playing. My attitude was, shall we say, pessimistic. The words cranky, glum, cynical, and downbeat clearly represented my posture, conversations, attitudes, and of course, thoughts. No book, no failure, I thought. I forced the writing onto paper, forgetting to attach any heart or ownership to this precious investment. Nearing six months of writing, I started telling others, and myself "this book is of no value. Books are a dime a dozen." Wrong. My reputation for quality work preceded me. Too many friends and acquaintances were not going to let me off the hook. I had a pre-sell list of anxious readers who believed in my ability to deliver what *they* needed to help them recharge.

Reflecting honestly, I admit my attitude isn't always positive. I ride the roller coaster of life just like many of my readers. And, I am painfully aware of the negative attitudes that erode my clear thinking and ability to make choices. Yet, when I proceed down that path of "Bad Attitude Annabel" too often, my awareness kicks in, I consciously reframe my attitude (of which I am in complete control), look at my choices from a different perspective, and go about determining what changes I am willing to make.

> *The greatest revolution in our generation is that of human beings, who by changing the inner attitudes of their minds, can change the outer aspects of their lives.*
>
> —Marilyn Ferguson

In the face of normal daily distractions, work, and family commitments, I eroded my own confidence by putting unrealistic time lines around this book. After enough mental and emotional electrical zingers to the head and heart, I began listening to my supportive friends, colleagues, and family. I didn't enjoy my "oh woe is me" attitude, even though I believed it was a safe haven to hide from responsibility to my readers and myself. Consciously, I took my own advice (and the playful chiding of my coach), and I set about to awaken each day with a prayer of thankfulness and at least one bright eye looking forward to the wonders of the day. I know I can write. Like *The Little Engine That Could*, "I think I can, I think I can." After all, I get to Recharge Women! How cool is that?

What attitude we choose to have from the first waking moment of each day determines whether it will be a miserable one filled with static electricity and unpleasant shocks, or a fruitful, pleasantly electrified day. It is a conscious choice. No one can take away our positive attitude unless, of course, we choose to give it up. We are at choice constantly. Our attitude and choices prompt our ability to see the possibilities for change—to brighten an entire room, not just a corner; to drive on the entire freeway of life, not just in the ruts.

Here are two activities I use to check my attitude and willingness to embrace choice and change. You may want to try them yourself.

Exercise—Snap

Place a rubber band on your wrist. Each time you notice a debilitating attitude, snap the band so that it hurts. Shift gears and replace a negative attitude with a positive one. Reward yourself for noticing (one of the first signs of change). Pain is avoidable. Each time the negative reappears, snap the band. It won't be long before you can happily shoot the rubber band across the room, launching the negative away. What if the negatives recur? Place another band on the wrist. You know the drill.

Exercise—Plus Or Minus

On the left column below are negative attitudes. Some may sound familiar. Cover the right side with a sheet of paper. For each negative you read, rewrite a positive on the paper covering the right side. When you are finished, uncover the right side and compare the prepared statement to what you have written. Add some of your own negatives in the spaces provided, especially as you become more aware of their existence. Write the reframed positive attitude on the right side. As awareness increases and you fire up your burning desire to recharge, the positive will override the negative. You deserve to live on the plus side of life, not the minus.

– Negative Attitude Statement –	+ Positive Attitude Statement +
I can't.	I can.
I'm so tired of caring for my mother.	I'm so blessed to have my mother in my life. While it's a lot of work, I'm choosing to enjoy my time with her and find one thing in the day that will help me appreciate our long-standing relationship.

– Negative Attitude Statement –	+ Positive Attitude Statement +
I don't wanna get up tomorrow.	I am excited to hear the birds, smell the fresh air, and thank God for the opportunity to be my best. I look forward to appreciating one new thing in my life.
This won't work.	I know there is a way for this to work. Let's see, who can help me figure this out? What are my resources?

The Recharged Woman knows when she strives for positive attitudes over negative, her self-worth and self-esteem skyrocket. More doors of opportunity and discovery open up for her. The possibilities for a hugely fulfilling life become evident. Positive attitudes are like a room full of light switches. Each one she turns on illuminates her magnificence a little more. Once she experiences how powerful and exhilarating it is to live in a positive light, the Recharged Woman wants to flip on more and more energy switches exposing more and more of life's perspectives and possibilities.

- What attitude do I choose?
- What doors does my attitude open (or close)?
- What are my negative triggers?
- How do I choose to deal with those triggers?

The Recharged Woman

- The Recharged Woman intertwines awareness of thoughts, behaviors, and feelings with a positive attitude. Awareness and attitude open doors to different perspectives and different ways of looking at a situation. This intertwining process fosters choice, change, deep personal fulfillment, and success. Awareness and attitude ignite the fire within.

- The Recharged Woman is pro-active in her approach to a positive attitude. She does a self-check regularly.

- The Recharged Woman consciously chooses her attitudes. Her attitudes are grounded in faith and a strong belief in herself. She is optimistic, sincere, and courageous. She is growth oriented, comfortable inside and outside her skin, and secure. Her attitudes are not dependent upon the judgments and opinions of others.

- The Recharged Woman refuses to submit to being a victim.

- The Recharged Woman consciously notices what triggers her emotions and thought processes, and chooses to reframe with a positive attitude. Attitude drives the way she perceives change and allows it into her life. Attitude promotes positive responses resulting in deep personal satisfaction.

Values, Our Guiding Lights

As self-awareness awakened within me, I began to feel more connected to my life. Yet, I realized that something was still out of sync. I did not have a clear vision of what created the squirmy stomach, the anxiety and neck tension, or the cloud of uncertainty that hung over many of my decisions and subsequent actions.

Aware that I am solely responsible for my unique attitudes and choices, I still find myself in occasional conflict. Sometimes that conflict is subtle like the faint flicker of a firefly darting about at dusk. Sometimes the conflict is very obvious, like walking into a field of thistle and thorny bushes, chasing a plethora of brilliant fireflies only to find myself in the midst of a lively beehive.

> *To do good things in the world, first you must know who you are and what gives meaning to your life.*
> —Paula P. Brown

Ouch! Ouch! Ouch! Imagine walking through that field of thistle, then impaling yourself on barbed wire.

By the time you slither into the bathtub to soak away the pain, you drop the portable phone into the tub and zap a nasty electrical shock down your spine. Phew! That's how I felt agonizing over this very chapter.

Truth telling, a personal value of mine, challenged my writing. Until I let go of the many definitions of values, I felt the stinging shock of conforming to everyone else's explanation of the word "values." Once I gained clarity over this dilemma, what seemed like draft number forty-seven zillion of this chapter found its way onto these pages. So, here's my definition and perception of what I believe is a major life-enhancing conductor to living the life you deserve—values.

At the core of what ignites the inner person is a unique and personal foundation of values. Values are not ethics in that ethics are contrived rules of conduct, often established by associations or organizations, for the purpose of setting standards of practice and behavior for its members. Values are not morals in that morals are influential lessons of character that portray generally accepted societal standards of right and wrong conduct. Values are not beliefs in that beliefs are something we perceive and accept as real and true, even when they might not be real or true. For example, I hold strong beliefs in God's ability to heal, even though I've never really seen God in person healing another human being. The world's inhabitants believe the earth is round even though most have never traveled into space to really see the earth from another vantage point. We have only seen the earth via pictures.

Values are not traits in that traits are surface characteristics, qualities, or features of a person or thing.

Let's also not confuse personal values with physical objects upon which we place value. Example: I value my car. It gets me where I need to go in a time efficient manner. (That is unless it is during rush hour or a Sunday afternoon when every gawker becomes a freeway turtle.) Just because I value the car, doesn't mean the car is a personal value ("things" are not values). I value the car because it provides a relatively efficient means of transportation. I accomplish more in less time.

I like to think of values as Guiding Lights. Guiding Lights are who we are, who we "be" from the inside out, not who we pretend to be when we are on public display. Values, or Guiding Lights, are our essence. They help us identify what's really important in our life. Guiding Lights clearly determine the land of "no kidding" where we create our own bottom line, where our rubber meets the road, and the line over which we will not cross. This is the inner place deep within us where we stand our ground over principles by which we live our daily lives. Guiding Lights values are the conduits that carry life's illuminating questions:

- What really matters?
- How does this decision really enhance the values by which I choose to live?
- Am I making excuses?
- For the sake of what, am I making this decision?

Guiding Lights are the bright white lights of "yes" that empower us to say "no" to temptation and conflict with grace, dignity, self-confidence, and deep inner commitment. Guiding Lights, or values, confer the passion of powerful conviction that overcomes fear, guilt, distraction, and doubt. They help ground us in balance, harmony, and a sense of peacefulness that reach from the tip of our nose to the curl of our toes.

As infants, we're born without significant knowledge. Our cradle of influence (parents, siblings, extended family, religious teachers, etc.) surrounds us with continuous learning. We observe and emulate values with each new experience. Influential people model for us a path of well-lit Guiding Lights. As critical tools for increased self worth, our values, or Guiding Lights, steer us in our decision-making. (Note: some values are more socially accepted than others. I do not place judgment on good or bad values. What we are exposed to is what we often emulate.)

As we mature, we test these engrained Guiding Lights against governing laws and the values of others. Most instilled values stick with us for life. As real life experiences increase, however, newer values sometimes replace the old. Just as a chiropractor realigns the spine to recharge a patient's energy, so too, must values be realigned when they no longer serve the person.

The family rogue, I was the mouthy kid, always questioning the status quo. I challenged more than one family value. Disrespectfully, I verbalized the word "no" about as many times as a toddler in his or her terrible twos. I was a teenager, though. "Prove it," "Who said?" and "Not in my lifetime," echoed continuously throughout my early teen years. New acquaintances, expanding travel opportunities, liberal viewpoints from teachers, and generally experiencing life outside my familiar community of influence clearly prompted conflict between the instilled values already incorporated in my life, and the tempting dark side of a seemingly exciting alternative way to live. (Okay, it sounds more ominous than it really was, but most teens and young adults experience increased independence and test their boundaries.)

Even though my intentions to test the status quo were well meaning, the directness with which I spoke often alienated me from the rest of the family. (Hey, I was a kid. I thought it was my job to make life challenging for my parents.) As I matured, I began to figure out that the squirmy stomach, tension, guilt, and anxiety over some of my decisions were directly related to my faltering values. In an attempt to dissolve peer pressures, I caved in to behaviors and actions that countered my Guiding Lights. At times I dumped discipline, depleted my dignity, cursed at character and commitment, and tipped my hat to temptation. My insides were churning 24/7.

In the short-run, I lost. I lost respect from those I loved. I bartered my identity to the opinions and judgments of others. I sabotaged my ability to be unconditionally happy, to live from a life of truth, to revere, respect, and honor that which makes me who I am from the inside out. I was a "wanna be."

Thankfully I was getting strong internal messages that something was amiss. I actually grew tired of fumbling around in the dark and feeling unsettled. Supported by the family and influential others who modeled and taught me my Guiding Lights (and who were anxious to point out my challenges), I changed my behaviors, choices, and actions to align more succinctly with my values. Even though many of my new decisions and actions weren't always fun and immediately gratifying (and they definitely weren't always popular amongst my peers), I felt better in the long run. I started trusting my ability to make choices from the values that were really important to me. I learned to say "no," to walk away from compromising situations, and to stand firmly in my values-based commitments.

Believe me, the temptations to waiver from my Guiding Lights still park on my doorstep today. Do I choose to pursue my income-generating career or commit to a more flexible schedule for my family? Do I choose the new position of chauffeur and sports mom over my beloved, personally gratifying role as a tenured ski instructor? Do I volunteer in service of others or work out in service of my own health? Do I sleep in on a damp, rainy morning or nurture my soul in worship of my faith? Do I move my ailing parent to a care facility or make space at home? Do I compromise sleep in order to get just one more chapter completed on this book knowing that I have an important meeting the next day that requires my full attention? Do I hold firmly to the house rules or bend them for a teenager just this one time? What conflict tempts compromise in the face of my Guiding Lights?

Life is a challenge. If it was not a challenge, I certainly wouldn't be writing this book, and you would most likely not be referencing this material. Truth be told, life constantly taps us on the shoulder. It often tackles us from behind. Just when we've cleaned up the last mess, changed the last diaper, tucked in a loving parent for a good night's rest, answered the last plaguing question from a coworker, that lumpy brown stuff hits the fan one more time. Choices are not always easy to make, *and* they are easier to make when weighed against the values we place in the forefront of how we want to live. Clarity of and commitment to Guiding Lights reduce conflict and compromise and increase personal direction, decision-making, and inner peace and fulfillment.

So what happens when two of our own Guiding Lights conflict with each other? How might we waiver without giving up one value for the other? There's no hard and fast rule. One of my coaching clients prioritized her two values. Then she looked at how she could incorporate some of the second value with the more important value. This client went on to say that on another occasion, the reverse decision might be made. Situations, then, can determine which Guiding Light takes precedence over the other.

Another client looked seriously at whether one of her Guiding Lights was really serving her anymore. Upon closer examination, she determined that the second conflicting value had to be eliminated from her list. What a great discovery on her part. A third coaching client redefined her two conflicting values into one more meaningful value.

Exercise—Guiding Lights

Defining Guiding Lights is, for some, a challenging task. It requires honest truth telling about what matters most to you. Here is an exercise that I use with my coaching clients to illuminate the most important values.

On a sheet of paper, list at least ten, but no more than twenty, personal values, your Guiding Lights.

Once you list your values, define more clearly what each one means to you. There are no right or wrong answers. The definitions are your perception of the Guiding Lights that represent the magnificent person you are and the way you choose to foster a fulfilling life.

(Stuck? If you promise not to adopt any "wanna have" values that are not really, truly yours, you can look for ideas in the back of the book.)

Great Work!

Next, prioritize your values in order from most important (#1) to least important (#10). Then ask yourself:

- What value(s) do I compromise regularly?
- What value(s) need(s) more conscious attention?
- How will I accomplish that?

Here are a series of defining and recharging questions designed to help you evaluate the choices you make.

- Will this choice and subsequent action move me closer to, or farther away, from living honestly with my value(s)?
- If I move further from living with my honest values, then what really matters?
- Am I selling out?
- If I move closer to living with my values, what do I know to be true about my decision? On a scale of one to ten (ten being the highest), how does this decision allow me to feel?

The Recharged Woman

- The Recharged Woman knows fulfillment and success can only be realized when her Guiding Lights are clearly written and understood, taken into account during decision-making, and honored on a daily basis.

- The Recharged Woman knows when her authentic, genuine self will shine through all the temptations that might otherwise corrode her Guiding Lights and lifestyle.

- The Recharged Woman knows her inner peace is dependent upon defining her values AND, most importantly, living her life according to those Guiding Lights.

- The Recharged Woman knows her Guiding Lights ignite her self-esteem and build integrity. Her choices, especially the difficult ones, provide a place for her to take a stand in her life without the guilt often associated with unpopular choices.

- The values-driven Recharged Woman casts away guilt over her choices because the opinions and judgments of others no longer paint her life's picture.

Plug Into Purpose

Are you passionate about becoming an expert at something, teaching others, helping others, solving problems, or using creative muscle to take ideas into action? Are you drawn to physical activities? Do you craft with your hands? Is nature a draw for you? Do you intuit or do you prefer to research the hard facts? Do you enjoy solitude to ponder and meditate, or is there an innate need to be with others? Do you sense one's feelings or observe one's actions? Are you creative or do you engage in analyzing everything? Do pictures, sounds, or words spark you? What is your passion? What is your purpose?

What we see depends mainly on what we look for.

—John Lubbock

Purpose is the inner voice that speaks to passion, that which fulfills our innermost needs. It is that internal heart space of knowing who we "be" as a person. Coupled with personal values, purpose is what drives us to be truly alive. Purpose breeds infectious enthusiasm. Look for the gravitational pull to certain people and activities in life. Feel the gravitational pull from within. Purpose is that twinge of excitement, the energy burst, and the electric light switch toggled to the ON position.

Purpose has significance in all we do. It explains why we do what we do. Without purpose, life becomes foggy. Life's sizzle fizzles. Without the foundation of purpose, we have little energetic drive to discover what life has to offer, let alone chart a path of positive lasting change.

Purpose gives meaning to life's activities. It pushes us to get up in the morning and enriches our communications with others. Richard J. Leider, in his book, *The Power of Purpose*, defines purpose as "the conscious choice of what, where, and how to make a positive contribution to our world." Further, Leider says the three themes that older adults expressed when interviewed about living life over again were "be more reflective, be more courageous, be clear earlier about purpose."

Discovery and definition of purpose evolve over time. The declaration "I'm a Mom" is purpose enough for some women, and synonymous with drudgery for others. In my twenties and thirties, my purpose, aligned with my values, was clearly that of being the best wife and mom I could be (although on really stressful days I second-guessed that idea more than once). As my son matured and his need for motherly wisdom and guidance lessened, so did my need to re-evaluate my purpose.

- How about you?
- Are you living the life you really want to live?
- What's your purpose in life?
- What lights your fire and turns your gloomy days into sun-filled splendor?
- On a scale of one to ten, ten being the highest, how meaningful is your life?
- What will it take to bump it up to a ten?

Ready, set, plug into purpose! Now that you are committed to embracing a positive attitude, you are more aware of how you impact yourself and others. You are aligned with your values. The next step is to plug purpose into becoming the Recharged Woman. Here are some ideas to help you get started.

Exercise—Purpose Statement

1. List what you love about you and life. Look for a common thread. Be truthful about what you need in life to be content and joyfully fulfilled.
2. Another way to unlock gifts and talents is to discover what people notice about you. When do you glow from the inside out? Notice what makes you smile. Notice where and when you get energized.
3. List any activities and feelings that absolutely discharge you.
4. Craft your purpose into a statement. Several methods follow. Choose one that works well for you.

Metaphor

I am the _____(thing)_____ **that** _____(action)_____
so that _____(benefits to you and others)_____.

An example might be: I am the *sun's warmth* that *melts the snow-capped mountains* so that *you might reveal your purpose and potential.*

I am the *catalyst* that *ignites the Recharged Woman in you* so that *you will be blessed with the best life possible.*

Phrase

If metaphors challenge you, try visualizing how your purpose comes into play using a similar phrase.

I _(do something or am someone)_ **so that** _(impacting result)_.

An example might be: I *coach others* so that *they might enjoy life at a deeper level.*

I *write books and speak publicly on the Recharged Woman* so that *others can have a less stressful and more fulfilling life (like mine).*

Dream

Another way to unlock purpose is to build a dream.

If I could do anything, it would be _____.

If I could be anyone, I would be _____.

Legacy

Perhaps it is easier to think in terms of leaving a legacy.

If I died tomorrow, how would I want to be remembered?

Job Description

From a "job" perspective, write a job description of the ideal position for you that blends career and personal life.

Contribution

From a contribution standpoint, try this statement:

What I can contribute to others while embracing my own worth is...

Feel any energy yet? Are you having a light bulb moment? Are there any thoughts or feelings knocking at your window of opportunity? Remember, a purpose statement is a work in progress. Of most importance is that you just *be* an active part of the journey that takes you toward discovering your unique gifts and talents.

The Recharged *Woman*

- The Recharged Woman is defined by her purpose.

- The Recharged Woman is clear about her purpose. From here forward, she dismisses activities that deplete her energy. Instead, patience prevails in redirecting her thoughts and actions that support her life purpose, gifts, and talents.

- The Recharged Woman is reflective. She consciously lives within her purpose and values. She takes time to reflect on the activities that support her mission and discards those that waste her potential.

- The Recharged Woman is courageous. Her purpose is her personal guidepost. She values and trusts her intuition to help reveal her truths. She is confident enough to dismiss any judgments that others may have toward her mission.

Balancing Life's Power
Surges and Brown *Outs*

I will never forget the dull scraping sound of wood dragging across hardened concrete. I will never forget the feel of my tender, bare skin careening across that same cold, steel-gray concrete as it deposited chunks of elbow and shreds of palm and knuckle along the path of defeat. Lastly, I will never forget the thud of my head against the unforgiving cement and the headache that followed.

A mere eight inches above the ground, precariously perched on a 10" x 30" slab of wood, I was practicing for the upcoming ski season. The board, when balanced properly, shifted back and forth resting on a tube-like cylinder that rolled along the floor. In need of improved balance, I fearlessly climbed aboard. Knees bent forward and arms extended like a soaring eagle, I moved left, then right, then left again shifting

The greatest gift that you can give yourself is a little bit of your own attention.

—Anthony J. D'Angelo

my weight like skiing a slalom course. For a moment I dreamed I was former Olympic star, Suzy Chaffee. Ta-da! Oops!

Never had I fallen so hard. Never. Does it matter that the last time I spent any significant number of hours on a balance board I was in my twenties and this time I was nearly fifty?

Balance is an incredible God-given gift. It keeps us upright as we single-handedly prepare dinner holding a squirming toddler on our hip. It enables us to walk with poise, steadily ride a bike, and confidently challenge a balance board.

Balance is tricky, though. Sustaining it requires constant adjustments. Sometimes the adjustments are small, almost incrementally unnoticeable changes. Sometimes the adjustments are huge. Scar tissue on my head, knuckles, and elbows attest to that truth.

Balance isn't *just* about our ability to keep from physically falling over. In recent years, the "B" word has been identified with the makeup of our life. It is our ability to juggle innumerable responsibilities and still maintain a sense of satisfaction. It challenges our ability to adjust to continuing change in all conduits of our non-static life.

Do everything in connection.
—Ed Shea

Balance is about equilibrium. A huge power surge in one area of life produces a brown out in other areas. For years, I lived a life of power surges and brown outs. I charged through the day, bounding out of bed with drive and ambition. I scurried through the morning motions without thought, moving on to the next series of events. Do this. Do that. Check off as many items on the list as possible. "Oh, you need that too?" I chimed politely. "Here, I'll just add it to my list." I said "yes" to just about everyone and everything. I answered to everyone but myself, and I did not realize I engaged in life from that perspective.

Driven by circumstance, I freely gave up my choices. I also gave up control of my own life, even though I began each day with good intentions to care for me. Exhausted by day's end, I felt great about having been a friend to others, having done a good job at work, and having been effective in most of the family matters. Yet, I short-changed my overall satisfaction in various life conduits.

Surroundings/Living Conditions
Family and Friends
Significant Other
Career/Professional Growth
God
Personal Growth
Money/Financial Reserves
Self/Self Care/Health
Fun/Recreation/Social Life
Life

Conduits of Life = Life's Balance Wheel

There are nine conduits, each representing a key element in life. God, or a Higher Power, is the center conduit from which all other conduit elements cultivate and balance together. Each conduit is dependent upon the other for lasting and deep fulfillment. While we never reach full sustainable balance, we naturally seek overall stability by continuous adjustments in our conduits. Our goal is to recognize when we are moving away from balance, check the satisfaction rating, adjust, and shift back toward it.

How do we put our life into balance? Simply put, look at what's working and what's not. Consciously be attuned to what must remain in our life and what must go. Be aware of why we decide what stays and how it aligns with our values and purpose. The practice of balancing our life necessitates we make some difficult, perhaps unpopular, decisions.

Exercise—Conduits of Life

Each conduit is measured in terms of personal satisfaction. On a scale of one to ten, ten being the highest satisfaction level achievable, choose a number that represents your personal satisfaction within one of the life conduits. For example, what is your satisfaction level with your significant other? With your career? With your home life or working conditions? Do this exercise for all nine conduits. If the numbers are consistently between seven and ten, life is pretty balanced. If the numbers waiver between five and seven, take a deeper look at what's not working. If any of the numbers falls below five, there is a definite imbalance in the life conduit(s). When you discover the imbalance, ask yourself these questions:

- Where am I out of balance?
- What suffers as a result of this imbalance?
- What other conduits suffer because of this imbalance?
- What am I focusing on within my Conduits of Life that diminishes the value of the other conduits?
- What do I need to change in order to serve my values, better balance my life, and feel more successful?
- Where do I over-promise and under-deliver?

The Recharged *Woman*

- The Recharged Woman seeks balance in all aspects of her life. She is keenly aware that life balance is something to work toward.
- The Recharged Woman acknowledges that the Conduits of Life are integrated, not compartmentalized. Activities in each conduit affect the others.
- The Recharged Woman notices the cues indicating her life is tilting out of balance.

Short *Circuits*

Our Main Switches give us the
foundation for lighting our path
to the Recharged Woman in all
of us. Yet, sometimes that path
of energy is interrupted by short
circuits in our lives. Short circuits cause us to get stuck in the
"OFF" position of life. They cause
us to waiver or flicker in our
commitment to a quality of life
that is meaningful and truly fulfilling. The short circuits
addressed in this section are
fear, guilt, and grief.

Pull the Plug on Irrational Fear

Whether we are an already anxious Annie, terrified toe-tappin' Theresa, extremely edgy Erin, jumpin' Jillian, queasy Quinella, or pitter-patter heart-pounding Pam, it is our own fear that pulls our energy plug out of the wall socket and diffuses life like an East Coast power outage. We all experience it at different levels throughout our lifetime.

Fear comes and goes during our lifetime. When faced with an unknown, our fear seems to rear its ugly head. It creates anxiousness, pounds at our chest with immediacy, and sends a flip-flop sensation to our tummy. Fear is good when it stops us and requires us to evaluate good from evil. When our safety is jeopardized, fear is a good emotion. Healthy fear protects us.

Sometimes healthy fear turns obsessive and irrational. For some individuals, a mental health specialist can guide the unhealthy fears back to normalcy. For most of us, however, our unhealthy, irrational fears are minimal enough that our own strength and willpower overcome this temporary adversity.

Whether we call it dread, horror, fright, panic, alarm, trepidation, apprehension, worry, anxiety, concern, or fear, when it keeps us from living a healthy, productive, and rewarding lifestyle, fear needs to be minimized. F.E.A.R.—False Evidence Appearing Real, stops us cold in our tracks, unplugs our electricity, and undermines feelings of success and self-esteem. Its capability to short-circuit our fulfillment in life is further enhanced by its invisibility. When we allow it, fear becomes powerful and it rests deep within our bones. We are often unaware of its presence as it affects our career, family, relationships, money issues, faith, personal development, self-care, and health. Irrational fear is a "head game," comprised of self-defeating ruminations.

> *You gain strength, courage, and confidence by every experience in which you really stop to look fear in the face. You are able to say to yourself, 'I have lived through this horror. I can take the next thing that comes along.' You must do the thing you think you cannot do.*
>
> —Eleanor Roosevelt

Anxiety and worry build in concert. We believe we lose control of the rational. In panic, we often blame others as a means to justify our fear. We shirk responsibility for our thoughts and actions.

Fear wears many masks. The most common masks of fear include:

- Procrastination
- Embarrassment
- Perfection
- Fear of Success
- What If's
- Losing Control
- Failure

"Procrastination" is the mask of putting off until tomorrow what we can accomplish today. Perhaps we are afraid of failing, or "being judged not good enough." Perhaps there is a concern for embarrassment or knowing the completed project won't be perfect. The mind chatters relentlessly until anxiety over what *might* happen (remember we cannot predict the future) increases to an overwhelming level.

The mask of "embarrassment" is evident when we allow someone else to ruffle our feathers, make us feel uncomfortable, self conscious, or ashamed. Thought patterns are disrupted, confusion sets in, cheeks flush, and that queasy feeling takes center stage. Our own fear of being embarrassed flips our light switch to OFF. Our risk-taking activities reduce significantly, if not halt altogether.

The mask of "perfection" declares that anything and everything must be perfect. We conjure up fears of failure, being judged, and losing status. We circle back to the mask of procrastination as a way to buy time for the perfect result that never arrives.

"Fear of success" is another debilitating mask. It precludes that when we accomplish all we set out to do, we still won't be satisfied or gratified even after our goal is reached. It's also the fear that we do not deserve to attain and sustain any successful growth as a result of reaching our goal. Fear of success attacks any self-worth that addresses our capabilities, and our deserving to be successful. It reduces us to "less than." Success comes from change. Because people fear the unknown factors connected to change, the comfort of status quo goes away. Fear of the unknown sabotages our forward actions.

The "what if's" mask presupposes disaster. "What if's" second-guess the worst-case scenarios yet to be determined. They also try to predict the future. They build walls of doubt as high as the eye can see. The fear of aging, rejection, losing a loved one, being alone, or loss of income are common "what if's" that extinguish any sparks lighting the way to a fulfilling life.

Losing control is the "tidy-box" fear mask. Everything fits into a tidy box, neatly arranged. Life is a grand plan AND a micromanaged plan. Our trust in the other person's ability to live up to our standards is minimal. Even if there is more work involved, getting the job done ourselves is preferable to delegating. We shut out others from knowing all but the surface persona for fear of showing our vulnerability. We believe this lessens the chance of our losing control.

The "fear of failure" mask perpetuates the awful feeling associated with past failure. Disappointment, the ability to meet our goals, and the expectations of others settle us into complacency. We fear authority figures, taking leadership, being made fun of, being vulnerable, and the idea of losing. It's far less painful to stay in the same rut in the road than to risk failing, especially when someone else might witness our failure.

But wait! We *can* control our fears. Combating fear is far less frightening than living emotionally crippled our whole life. How many times have we confronted a fear, overcome it, and then said, "that wasn't so bad"? That's how it usually ends. As we conquer the fear, our helplessness is replaced with increased confidence, strength, satisfaction, and worth. Fear is not our enemy. How we *perceive* the fear is our mind game enemy.

The Recharged Woman looks at fear from a perspective of what she can control and what she cannot. She lets go of those things over which she has no control. She does not focus on the "what if's" and events in the future that might happen, but rather focuses on the here and now. The Recharged Woman asks "what's the worst thing that can happen, and can I live with that outcome?"

Exercise—Short Circuiting Fear

The following steps work toward eliminating irrational fear.

1. Acknowledge the fear. Create a self-inventory. Keep a journal, whether written or audio, to help you notice where and when the fear shows up. Use it also to acknowledge that you are moving in a positive direction the majority of the time. Be honest with yourself. What are the fears that run your life? Write down all the things, events, and people about which you hold some fear (failure to pass a class, trust, heights, making mistakes, or being criticized). Determine if the fear is real or imagined. Then write about how this fear captures your life and suffocates or sabotages it and how that makes you feel. If you weren't afraid, what would you do, how would you feel? Who could you be?

2. Look at surrounding stimuli that may be attributing to fear. Get enough rest and relaxation. Choose supportive relationships carefully. Avoid caffeine, nicotine, and alcohol. Notice where your confidence ends and imagined fear begins.

3. Change what you can about the fear. You know you cannot control all of the circumstances around you. You cannot control others or their actions, opinions, and judgments. You cannot predict the future. You cannot change the past. What you can control is your

reaction to others and the circumstances that surround your life. You can control your thoughts, actions, what you say, your gifts and talents, how you use your time, and how you associate with others.

4. Let go of the rest. Unconditionally accept that today you have done your best and you are an excellent person. When you don't beat up on yourself, you can actually like you, become more confident, relaxed, and prideful.

5. Break the vicious, negative cycle by engaging in a physical activity that helps refocus. Run, bike, clean, telephone a friend, sing, play the piano. Purposefully engage in a positive diversion.

6. Share your fear with someone. Help gain perspective. Create realistic expectations for yourself. Create the attitude of "can do" and "I'm in control of what I control." Teach others you trust to help you notice your fears. Entrust them to tell the truth about what they notice you fear.

By the sheer virtue of being a human being, the emotion we call "fear" is a part of our life. We can allow it to minimize and shape our existence, or we can face it and overcome it, thus opening up rich experiences and limitless possibilities for an abundantly fulfilling life. We get to choose.

Here are some questions to challenge your irrational fear.

- I am worried about what?
- The voice of fear tells me what?
- What does the voice of courage and conviction tell me?
- If I weren't afraid, what would I do?
- If I weren't afraid, how might I feel?
- What is the worst thing that can happen if I face my fear?
- What is the likelihood that the worst will happen?
- Can I live with that outcome?
- What realistic expectations and goals do I need to create for change to occur?
- Who will encourage me and hold me accountable to making this change?
- What are the rewards I will receive?
- What imagined fear do I commit to conquering?

The Recharged Woman

- The Recharged Woman deciphers between healthy, rational (real) fear and the negative, irrational (imagined) one.

- The Recharged Woman looks at fear from a perspective of what she can and cannot control.

- The Recharged Woman lets go of those things over which she has not control.

- The Recharged Woman trusts herself enough to take the risks necessary to reduce and/or eliminate her imagined fear.

- The Recharged Woman asks "what's the worst thing that can happen if I face this fear, and can I live with that outcome?"

Zap *Guilt*

On a recent adventure to the Mall of America, I took time out for a break. I swear I had walked ten miles, my eyes shifting from store to store, ogling at fashion, imagining a new hairstyle, dreaming of a new bedroom ensemble, and mentally measuring my living room wall for a new piece of art. As I settled into a very comfortable chair, packages by my side, a cool beverage in my hand, guilt flew in my face. "What if I spent too much money today?" "I should have stayed at home to clean house instead." I heard the message, "you don't need new clothes. The old ones are just fine." Then I heard the other message, "no matter how nice your clothes are, they will never be the right fashion statement, but go ahead and try it anyway." Oh boy, here I go again. I might as well be riding on the carousel at Camp Snoopy in the Mall of America. Circling in front of my view, the clearly visible, brightly colored, and engagingly enticing ride reminded me of the same

Life is not a stress rehearsal.
—Loretta Laroch

well-worn phrases of guilt spinning around in my head over and over and over again.

But this time, I recognize the familiar gremlins of guilt. Ah-ha! Gotcha! I mentally shift my thoughts and magically invite them onto the carousel. Gone! I've sent them away to get dizzy all by themselves. I return to sipping my cool beverage, softening my facial tension into a warm, relaxed, and inviting smile, and realize I deserved to treat myself to a day of shopping. I spent less than my budget, I know the clothes look nice and fit me well, and I really don't need the opinions and judgments of others to determine whether I'm a fashion plate or not. I used to believe I could not hop off the carousel of guilt. Then I realized that I held the power of focus to turn off the negative energy, stop the self-defeating circling of wild horses, and step off freely.

Guilt. We own it, live with it; sometimes I think we love it. It's a place of least resistance—a place not to own our own feelings or declare our unique needs. It's a place where we avoid responsibility. Here is a tough truth—it is a place of choice.

What is guilt? It is not conscience in that conscience is the sense of right and wrong within us. Conscience tells us what is wrong and keeps us from doing it. Further, it tells us what is right and leads us to do it. Guilt is the state of having committed a crime (usually with deliberateness) or violated a law. The condition implies intentional engagement in a criminal activity thus deserving of blame or guilt.

The guilt to which we are referring in this chapter is based on feelings of inadequacy. Society has labeled these feelings as guilt. The guilt we have become so accustomed to carrying on our shoulders is not about our actions. It is about our feelings and emotions. There becomes increased confusion between our incorrect actions (not intentionally designed to hurt others) and the feeling of unworthiness as a result of a wrong action. When the action is done with a positive intention and without self-interest, it is not to be equated with guilt even if the action is done incorrectly. Making mistakes is normal. Learning from the mistakes and making corrections moves us toward personal success. Freedom from feelings of guilt begins by trusting that our actions are well intentioned.

Where did guilt first rear its ugly head? Our influential circle of grandparents, parents, siblings, teachers, and friends all imposed their values, opinions, judgments, and fears upon us. Often the guilt was subtle and suggestive in its message. Other times the feelings of guilt were thrust upon us, passed on to us, slowly injected into our veins like a slow-moving poison, until it became so much a part of us that we became masters of guilt. Perhaps in the culture in which you grew up mothers and fathers were taught by their parents "to be strong," "big girls don't cry," "move on, you'll get over it," "don't feel bad," "suck it up; it's your responsibility," "be brave," "you can't fall apart," and "it's not that bad." Well intentioned as that advice may have been, it rejected the notion that our feelings were an integral part of who we were as an individual. When we didn't fit into that mode of behavior, we were taught to feel guilty.

As time went on, others imposed guilt upon us by reinforcing our already fragile and negative self-perception. Still others built in our minds false scenarios of misdeeds whereby we were continually at fault. They imposed a right way by which we were to live, one that was unrealistic and usually challenged our values. We existed in a state of constant uncertainty. We never knew if we measured up. We never knew if we had arrived at a place of approval, so we continued to circle for more, to strive to arrive, but we never landed. The more we did, the more there was to do. Life's burdens piled up into a guilt-ridden existence. We conformed to others while giving up our needs, passions, and soul. We complied to "fit in." The unhealthy relationship with the manipulator of our feelings was shallow, and at best was designed to beat us down while building up the other person (never to expose their interpersonal weaknesses).

Love yourself first and everything else falls into line.
—Lucille Ball

Our self-talk screamed at us. "I do not deserve," "it is my fault," "I am responsible either way," "I must never let down my guard," "there is only one right way," "others should never suffer," "if others (like family) fail, it is my responsibility," "others expect me to," and "their judgment of me is critical and valid."

Individuals of significance in our life naturally taught us what was taught to them. A chain reaction of denial of emotions and feelings became the norm from generation to generation. "Don't do that. Shame on you. You're no good if you don't…."

Having chiseled away at our worth, when our self-esteem was the least bit tarnished, it was common to seek the approval of others. After all, at this point, we weren't praised, complimented, or recognized for any of our accomplishments. We gave up our identity to please others by adhering to their judgments and opinions. Suppressing feelings for the sake of belonging and being accepted was one of the many disguises of guilt. We quickly learned that negative self-talk reinforced guilt, and we became experts at it. Guilt was also a safe place to avoid confrontation, so we often succumbed to the expectations of others.

A jolting bolt of guilt lightning that knocked us to the ground was the CSW—"coulda, shoulda, woulda." The CSW lifestyle was far from perfect. A discharged woman kept going back in time to punish herself for her interpretation of a less than perfect outcome. She pondered past experiences where she believed she "coulda, shoulda, woulda" done something differently or been someone different from who she really was.

How often do we feel guilty because we aren't perfect in our thoughts and actions? Plenty of times. Just like the "hindsight is 20/20" theory, when we allow perfection to get in the way of doing our best and accepting that our best is excellent, we enter the land of "coulda, shoulda, woulda."

"I shoulda (should have) been there."

"I coulda (could have) done a better job."

"I coulda (could have) given up my tickets to the opera."

"I woulda (would have) been there, but I didn't know…"

The self-talk of "If only's" evolved into more nasty, crossed wires that short-circuited our ability to live in the present. "If only" was a phrase that often followed "why." "If only" offered us a place to wallow in guilt and self-punishment. "If only I had listened." "If only I had been more supportive." "If only I had tried a little harder." I'm sure you can create your own list. The truth is: what is now, is now. The past is past. "If only" cannot change the past or even yesterday's regrets. It can simply make us miserable as it robs us of our harnessed potential for increased self-worth, esteem, internal peace, and personal success.

How does it serve us (and our family) to feel guilty about the "coulda, shoulda, woulda's" and the "if only's"? It doesn't serve us well, so when will we drop them from our life?

"What if" is a great place to fabricate worry, anxiety, and guilt not only in the present but also, most assuredly, in the future. "What if" is about living to the perceived expectations of our self and others without regard for our needs. We begin to feel insecure about our decisions, our capabilities, and us. We will do almost anything to be accepted by others. As with other forms of guilt, we prostitute the inner soul of who we are. We let go of the core of our values. Our life focuses on "do more, be better, and please everyone at our own expense."

What do we accomplish by worrying about the future? How does it make us feel?

Just like a song we can't erase from our mind (my song is Disney's *It's a Small World*), guilt is a mental paralysis coming from an overactive conscience. Stuck in repetition of negative, self-defeating, nagging thought, we feel that something is wrong with us. We develop an overactive conscience.

The overactive conscience has an innate need to meet the expectations of others (not our own expectations) for the sake of gaining approval because of our own insecurities. If we keep selling out to others, we wrongly believe we are an asset to that person. Unfortunately, this is an empty, dark hole we are crawling into. We cannot be truly happy without meeting our own expectations first.

Guilt, worry, suppression of feelings, and anxiety are certain to discharge a woman and empty her fuel source. The Recharged Woman learns she cannot control the thoughts and actions of others. She can, however, keep the thoughts of others at bay. She does not have to buy into guilt provoking actions of others. In fact, the Recharged Woman is free to eliminate many of those negative nay sayers. The negative ninnies still around can be quieted with such phrases as "I acknowledge your opinion." Then throw the opinion away. When clearly focused on her values, the Recharged Woman limits her exposure to irrational thoughts that tend to corrupt the truth. When her anxiety elevates, she reframes her thinking, looking at what she can and cannot control and adapts positively. The Recharged Woman deems herself worthy. She acknowledges her excellency in all she does and embraces her attitudes and accomplishments. Perfection is unrealistic. Excellency brings out the finest in her.

Exercise—Guilt Less

In helping clarify where you are with guilt, answer the following questions.

- What feeling of guilt blocks me from moving forward in my life?
- What am I doing to make this problem worse for myself?
- What would this issue look like if I chose to feel no more guilt?
- What part of it can I control?
- How does it relate to my values and purpose in my life?
- How do I feel about that?
- Where do I draw the line?
- What do I choose to change?

The Recharged *Woman*

- The Recharged Woman chooses to take responsibility for her thoughts, feelings, and actions. She refuses to enter into the blame game. She differentiates between the truth and irrational thoughts.

- The Recharged Woman limits her exposure to irrational fears, worry, anxiety, and guilt. She honors her values and lives in truth.

- The Recharged Woman recognizes when her anxiety elevates and takes conscious responsibility and action to reframe her thinking. She notices what triggers her anxiety, evaluates whether or not she can control it, and adapts her perspective to serve her in a positive manner.

- The Recharged Woman is aware that while others may want to impose feelings of guilt upon her, only she can impose them upon herself. She chooses not to feel guilty. She is a confident woman in her own right.

- The Recharged Woman celebrates freedom from guilt. She deems herself worthy. She acknowledges her excellency in all she does and embraces her attitudes and accomplishments. Perfection is unrealistic. Excellency brings out the finest in her.

- The Recharged Woman surrounds herself with individuals who support her efforts. She chooses to leave behind those who judge her and attempt to suppress her feelings and impose guilt. She does not allow others to manipulate her.

- The Recharged Woman stops negative self-talk. Even though she cannot control the circumstances and events taking place around her, nor can she control the thoughts, actions, opinions, and judgments of others, she chooses to control *her* reactions. She is consciously in control of herself.

The Courage to Grieve, Then Move *On*

My beloved dog, Duchess, a sleekly built but always drooling boxer, died suddenly. Gretta von Goldfish died, too. She got the royal flush. Mom helped bury Pete the parakeet. He probably still lies in a tissue-lined shoebox under the big red bush on the southeast corner of my childhood home. The wheel of my favorite doll buggy fell off in the quiet, tree-lined street just a few houses away from the watchful eyes of my mother. The carriage tipped over. My brand new doll, Chatty Cathy, suffered a scratched face in the most unfortunate accident. Those early childhood losses were so-o-o traumatic at the time. From my experience level and current perspective today, though, I wish life's recent tragedies were all that small and manageable.

> What lies behind us and what lies before us are tiny matters compared to what lies within us.
>
> —Ralph Waldo Emerson

Grieving occurs when we experience loss—loss of a loved one, loss of a job, loss of a child going off to kindergarten or college, loss of a material possession that breaks or is missing, or a friend moving to another part of the country. The intensity and longevity of the grief varies as to the depth and breadth of the impact of the loss. Grieving over a broken vase or favorite candy dish may last a few hours to a few days. Grieving over the loss of a loved one may last for many months, tapering to lesser degrees of grieving over a period of years.

Grief, while natural, is a short-circuit that depletes our energies like unplugging the light bulb by which we are guided down a dark hallway. This chapter is not meant to cover all aspects of grief. Nor is it designed to be supportive through the grieving process. There are many books and support groups that address this issue. This chapter's purpose, though, is to bring awareness that grief drains energy. Acknowledge its presence. This chapter also brings awareness of what to look for when ready to move forward and recharge your new life.

Losses come in small packages and large ones too. Each one initiates some sort of change in our life. Big losses include, but are not limited to, the death of a close friend or loved one. Overwhelming and intense grief brings with it a dramatic shift to a state of denial, emptiness, despair, and overwhelming confusion. It's difficult to envision what the future might look like. For some it might be difficult to envision tomorrow and what it might bring to our lives. It's easy to dwell in disappointment, anger, guilt, and self-pity. Resentment may turn into revenge. Quickly, life becomes a downward spiral into a path of constant negativity. On top of that, we've run out of energy!

The small packages or "little deaths," as grief expert Elisabeth Kübler-Ross calls them, are the less traumatic losses. Her writing suggests these experiences build the resiliency necessary to overcome larger losses. Little deaths might include the loss of a stolen family treasure like the ring Grandma gave us as a keepsake. Perhaps a favorite pet died, we failed a test in school, or lost a bid for a job promotion.

The resiliency we build from experiencing small losses allows us to recover more quickly from larger losses and the accompanying changes that follow. Each time we bounce back from a loss and the associated grief, we build stronger coping muscles. As we develop resiliency through experience, we tend to demonstrate more durability, flexibility, and optimism that things will get better. We also develop an openness to learn and live from other perspectives. We learn that while a loss can be very traumatic, resolving the issues around that loss lead to personal healing and an ability to go on and thrive versus merely survive. Resiliency requires us to pay attention to what's happening, how we're feeling, and how we are adapting to change. After all, life will never be the same.

Grieving is a convalescing period. The pain of loss undulates as we come to accept the changes in our life. There are periods of breakdowns when everything seems to come apart. Then there are periods of relative normalcy when we are more accepting of where we are in life. It is a time to notice where we are in the grieving process and accept it.

As you begin to notice yourself in the grieving process, be aware of the physical, emotional, and spiritual drain that occurs. I never equated grieving with courage, but I learned that it takes great courage to acknowledge one's mourning. It takes courage to be open and honest about our feelings. It takes courage to face the opinions and judgments of others and look inwardly for strength to stand up with confidence. It is the courageous person who knows she will cycle through grieving faster when she acknowledges and accepts her feelings rather than bury them in the face of denial or self-righteousness.

It takes courage to take care of ourselves in spite of the chaos and confusion thrust upon us in this emotionally delicate and distressing time. It takes courage to believe in a Higher Power and to trust the inevitable. It takes courage to fully experience and express our feelings. It takes courage to keep us from running away from our losses and the emotions and deep feelings that go along with them.

In the final phases of grief our minds and hearts begin to gain clarity around our abilities to surpass "survive" and begin to propel us into a lighted pathway called "thrive." When the recurring theme of messages in our head grants us a readiness to move forward, to get on with life, and to accept change, mere coping and surviving life no longer become the acceptable mode of existence. While life's purpose and meaning may yet be foggy for us, there is a definite inner push to move forward, to change what is no longer beneficial to our worth, our potential.

Sometimes the grieving process slows us down. Sometimes it stops us in our tracks. Either way, grieving is a part of life. It demands our attention and needs to be resolved over time. The Recharged Woman acknowledges and accepts that the grieving process discharges her. The Recharged Woman also acknowledges that as she transitions back into a more fulfilling and purposeful life, there are tools for recharging.

When sensing a readiness to move forward into a more recharged and enlightened life, ask these questions:

- What shift do I notice in my emotional strengths?
- What truths about change am I realizing and accepting?
- What more is there for me right now?

The Recharged *Woman*

- The Recharged Woman accepts loss and grief as a natural part of life.

- The Recharged Woman exhibits patience for and accepts the grieving process. She does not hide her feelings. Rather, she uses them to move her through the process in a compassionate, truthful, and healing way.

- The Recharged Woman overcomes any guilt or resentment aimed at her loss.

- The Recharged Woman has the personal resolve to move forward as grief diminishes. She views her life as a reinvention worthy of living.

- The Recharged Woman is willing to embrace hope, to recover, and to recreate a new life—in time.

Rechargers

Rechargers

As we reconnect the short circuits and continue to plug in,
power up, and switch on our
main switches, the following
chapters build upon and support
our foundation. These lightning
bolts of energy are filled with real
world, simple, and applicable
exercises to re-ignite the
Recharged Woman in each of us.
Also included are powerful,
thought-provoking, and action-
driven questions designed as cat-
alysts for recharging our head,
heart, body, and spirit.

Permission Granted to Move Forward

Asking permission is a respectful practice. "May I please be excused?" "May I help you?" Sometimes, however, we take the exercise to an unhealthy extreme. When we cross that line into unhealthy requests, especially those generated as a condition of guilt, we end up giving away our power and our control over our own lives. We lose confidence and self-esteem at being decision makers and in knowing our own capabilities. We lose our identity.

Yet, as women we struggle every day to take charge of our own lives. Section Two of this book pointed out how the many types of fear and guilt leave us drained and empty. For those of us who hesitate to step into Section Three and grab firmly onto the lightning bolts of energy, permission is granted to move forward.

The Recharged Woman ignites life with her own personal

The world rewards those who take responsibility for their own success.
—Curt Gerrish

decisions that are mentally, emotionally, physically, and spiritually healthy. She doesn't ask permission to be the woman she deserves to be. She accepts responsibility for it.

I will not let anyone walk through my mind with their dirty feet.
—Mahatma Gandhi

The process of getting strong from the inside out doesn't happen over night. We hesitate and wonder how well we can stand as accountable decision-makers of our own lives. As we light the fire within us, here is a smattering of other permissions. Consider using them as tools to eliminate the need to give away personal responsibility and control of our lives.

Permission is granted to:

- Give us permission not to ask for permission from others. That action gives veto power to someone else. We give away control of our choices.
- Quit. The saying "winners never quit" is bothersome. Winners are so attuned to the process of winning, that they quit what doesn't work. They quit the negative attitudes, self-defeating behaviors. They quit giving away their own power. They quit the stuff that does not work. This gives way to huge space for what does work well.
- Discover and declare our values—and live them with integrity and honesty.
- Seek our purpose.
- Live on purpose and with intention.

- Live with a take-charge attitude.
- Live life one day at a time.
- Work toward balancing all parts of our lives.
- Risk.
- Be fully present in the moment and enjoy its richness.
- Fuel our passion(s) and engage the passion in our lives.
- Say no to what doesn't matter.
- Say yes only when we can say no to something else on our full plate.
- Clear away life's distractions.
- Make the choices that bring us fulfillment.
- Zap guilt out of our lives.
- Grieve, and move on when the time is right.
- Face our greatest fears and extinguish their power over us.
- Express our feelings and thoughts and ask for what we need.
- Live confidently in our own truth.
- Respect what we need.
- Respect who we are.
- Make choices.
- Initiate and follow through on meaningful change.
- Choose to live life with a positive attitude.
- Let go of the opinions and judgments of others.

- Hire a success coach.
- Integrate emotions with thoughts and actions.
- Seek God and invest in Him.
- Establish meaningful relationships.
- Dump relationships that no longer serve our needs.
- Set clear personal boundaries.
- Affirm everything about us that is true—and believe it.
- Listen with intuition.
- Listen to our inner voice.
- Listen to the unspoken words.
- Love ourselves and be loved.
- Participate in extremely outrageous self-care.
- Wear our self-confidence from the inside out.
- Stop justifying.
- Know when we are falling out of balance in our lives.
- Acknowledge at least one greatness in our day and celebrate it.
- Tune into our lives and become aware of what works and what does not work.
- Overcome fear with the fire of life's possibilities.
- Discover contentment while pursuing and achieving meaningful goals.
- Be proactive in our lives.
- Define what success means to us.
- Begin to live life with intoxicating success.
- Feel free.

Phew! What a way to begin Section Three. I feel a load lifted off of my shoulders—definitely en*light*ened. How about you? Where are you granting permission?

The Recharged Woman

- The Recharged Woman uses the act of asking permission as a means to convey respect.

- The Recharged Woman accepts responsibility for her need to take charge of her own life by granting her own permission.

- The Recharged Woman ignites life with her own personal decisions that are mentally, emotionally, physically, and spiritually healthy.

I CAN say No!—Establishing
Clear Personal Boundaries

Life is a moment-by-moment navigational adventure that sometimes turns into a nightmare. Which way do I turn? What road is straightest and easiest to navigate? What surprise detour awaits me today? What road leads to a gas station? Help! I'm nearly out of fuel. My lights are dimming. I'm discharging and running on empty!

Without personal boundaries we over-promise and under-deliver. We succumb to circumstance instead of living by values-driven choice.

—Pamela Nelson

We're constantly pulled in a multitude of directions by friends, loved ones, co-workers, and the unwanted and unexpected interruptions that paralyze our ability to keep to a plan of action. We're discharged from answering the same questions that an elderly parent asks day after day; from chasing after the very children we agreed to enroll in multiple sports and arts programs; from taking care of everyone else in lieu of a long, hot, uninterrupted bubble bath or a workout. Lock us away, please, into a room with four soundproof walls and no telephone.

Monumental moments of learning that recharge the spirit are sometimes too close for comfort. Busily driving in moderate traffic, I scooted up right behind a slow-moving dump truck on the expressway. Unable to pass, I slowed up, keeping a safe distance behind the oversized, heavy load. The back of the truck displayed two strategically located arrows, one pointing to the left side of the truck (the passing lane) and the other pointing to the right side of the truck (the impassable shoulder of the freeway). The message printed below the left facing arrow read "passing side." The poignant message plastered below the right facing arrow shouted "suicide." Each day we make choices. Will today's decisions maneuver us into the passing side of life or recklessly swerve us onto the shoulder of certain harm and into the suicide of life? Will we discharge or recharge?

In a teeter totter world of being catapulted upwards or slammed downwards, we desperately need personal boundaries to cushion and balance the ride. Boundaries enable us to move into the passing side of life and avoid the suicide. For some, creating boundaries is finding simplicity. For others, it's organizing as many activities as possible into a place in time, yet doing so with intention, not by default of circumstance.

Boundaries shield us from getting lost in the daily shuffle. Whereas author Tom Peters coined the business phrase "underpromise; overdeliver," without personal boundaries we over-promise and under-deliver. We succumb to circumstance instead of living by sound, values-driven choice.

Having personal boundaries is like being in a well-lit room on a sunny day. We see the walls clearly. Living with a lack of boundaries is like groping in the dark for any wall surface that might serve as a guidepost. How do we know when our boundaries lose definition and grow fuzzy? We feel a loss in our ability to freely choose. We allow ourselves to be driven by circumstance. Like the chapter on guilt, the dreaded words echo loudly "I can't," "I need to," and "I have to." The fierce blame game soon takes effect. "I can't because….(it's someone else's responsibility, choice, or action)." The perspective of powerlessness is akin to mixing the deadly explosives of frustration, anger, guilt, fear, obligation, resentment, the feeling of being used, tension, and failure into one sizzling cocktail certain to short circuit and blow sky high. Internally, we resemble a pretzel bending in every direction except our own.

Relationships require mutual understanding of, and respect for, rules and guidelines, leading to clear boundaries. When we fail to set personal boundaries, we send a distinct message to those with whom we share a relationship. Without honest input, assumptions and expectations arise. Misunderstanding of verbal and nonverbal messages run rampant. We subtly teach others how to treat us. We ultimately send a silent message to others to create boundaries for us. We short circuit personal choice and responsibility. We become fair game for overuse by those with well-lit and clearly defined boundaries.

- How fair is it to you to live without boundaries?
- How satisfying is it for you to live without boundaries?
- How meaningful is it for others to define your boundaries?

Personally defined values are at the center of how we live. Boundaries become transparent when we lose perspective on our values (see Chapter Three). Once engrained in us, decision-making based on values is uncomplicated. When confronted with challenging or tempting choices surrounding the fringe of our boundaries, we look to our values to affirm those borders.

Setting boundaries is a kind and respectful way of letting others know our limitations based on our system of values. We make tough, sometimes unpopular decisions in order to strengthen our identity and recharge our lifestyle. The ability to set our boundaries helps others clarify their boundaries. It also contributes to a stronger and more respectful mutual relationship. Reverse the discharging thought process from "I can't say 'no,' and I don't have time for me because too many others have important needs," to "when I care for myself first, I have the mental, physical, spiritual, and emotional health to create strong boundaries to support myself and others."

Boundaries construct a safe place to say "yes" to what is truly important to us in the face of living within our personal values. Boundaries provide a safe environment to say "no" to those interrupters that do not serve us and extinguish the fire of life. Conditioned from poor choice making in a life without clearly defined boundaries, it is excruciatingly difficult to say "no." It is not always the popular choice in light of the fact that those around us are accustomed to our 24/7 availability. While we believe in the concept of helping others, without boundaries, we become taskmasters to everyone who asks more of us. Consider these questions:

- How healthy is it for others when I'm always available to them?
- What do they gain by engaging my services all the time?
- When will they step into responsibility and accountability to learn new skills and engage in responsibility sharing?
- What do I really want the relationship to feel like?

If saying "no" is difficult, then try memorizing the phrase "let me think about it and I'll get back to you." Articulating this statement buys time and reduces the urge to say "yes." It forms a boundary of time to regroup thoughts, weigh the costs and benefits of saying yes or no, and gently prepares the other person for the possibility of a firm "no." At decision time, we are not caught up in the emotional pull of the moment. We have had time to weigh the options privately and rehearse the answer. We are better able to stand firmly in the decision without compromise or apology.

The discipline of saying "no" is not designed to be a tool to repel others from long-standing relationships. Rather, it is designed as a doorbell to opportunity, not the doormat onto which others are stepping without regard for our needs. Whether life is like a paper plate or fine china, there are only so many yeses we can pile on our plate. The discipline of saying "no" enables us to balance the plate without personal collapse.

The following exercises are designed to help bridge the gap between awareness of choice and actually engaging in meaningful boundary setting.

Exercise—Say "No"

- Use a discerning eye and ear to evaluate where I say "yes" today.
  - What emotions are present?
- Use a discerning eye and ear to evaluate where I say "no" today.
  - What emotions are present?
- How many more times do I say "yes" than "no"?
- How full is my plate?
- How does each "yes" and "no" associate itself with my value system?
- Where do my boundaries exist now, and where do they need to be redrawn?
- What healthy boundaries am I creating for myself by saying "yes" to those needs that are most value

driven and ultimately peace producing and "no" to peripheral opportunities?

- How do I feel about that decision?
- For each "yes" to which I commit, how many "nos" do I commit to reduce from my list?
- Where am I carving out time for me?

Exercise—Two Times No

- Practice saying "no" twice as often as you say "yes."
- What do I notice?
- What do I like about this process?
- Where does this process work well for me?

Exercise—Buying Time

- Memorize the following statement
  "Let me think about it and I'll get back to you."
- Use it often.

Take charge of your life. Be responsible for drawing purposeful boundaries. Flip the power switch to ON.

- When I choose to say no, do I convey it with conviction and without excuse and/or guilt?
- What is really important to me?
- What needs to be different?
- What more in life do I want?
- What do I want to eliminate?

The Recharged Woman

- The Recharged Woman lives by values-driven choices. She is careful not to over-promise and under-deliver.
- The Recharged Woman is ultimately responsible for creating her own boundaries.
- The Recharged Woman draws her boundaries by saying "no" to what does not serve her values and purpose.
- The Recharged Woman creates healthy boundaries by limiting the number of "yeses" in her life to a manageable amount.

In the Moment...
Do-Be-Do-Be-*Do!*

Congratulations! You have just been promoted to the responsibilities of Meticulous Mom, Happy Housekeeper, Cheerful Chauffeur, Creative Chef (or Pizza Princess), Whirlwind Waitress, Loyal Employee (commonly referred to as Primary or Secondary Income Provider), Accounts Payable Specialist (Bill Payer), Wondrous Wife, Bodacious Bed Partner and Supreme Snuggler, Veteran Volunteer, Home Front Healer (Bandage Brigade), God Guide, Evening Prayer Participant, Weight Watcher (Flab Fanatic), Terrific Toilet Detoxifier, Athletic Events Supporter (Laundry Queen of athletic supporters, filthy socks, stinky shirts, and purple grape juice stains), Grocery Getter, FFO—Family Financial Officer, Primary Caregiver (Parental Protector), CFO—Chief Family Organizer—i.e. Kalendar

Love the moment,
and the energy of that
moment will spread
beyond all boundaries.
—Corita Kent

Keeper, AND Kitchen Komedian (keeps the family laughing when they realize you haven't shopped for three weeks).

With so many responsibilities, it's no wonder we disconnect from life in the midst of living it! With all we have to do, it's easy to discharge and short circuit. Our feet are hard-charging down the sidewalk, our minds are sorting our thoughts, and our life is completely task-oriented. Some might say it's a real "do-do" life! Robots we are not. Yet amidst all we do, our satisfaction that comes at day's end is often minimal, at best.

The Recharged Woman is a "Do-Be-Do-Be-Do" Woman.
—Pamela Nelson

Engaging exclusively in the "doing" of activities leaves us void of experiencing all the senses that make us whole and serve our greater purpose.

We live with the false assumption that more is better. The more we have on our calendar, the more involved and better we think we are at parenting. The more we do at work, the more we think we "position" ourselves for the future. The more we do for others, the more we think we are judged as giving and philanthropic. But where is the satisfaction we are supposed to be receiving from this blur of a life? More is better, but only when we feed ourselves from the inside first.

Stop! Stop "doing" and start "being."

In Chapter One we learned that personal awareness is key to eliciting conscious and lasting change. This chapter narrows the focus to capturing life "just in time," "right now," and "in the moment." Connecting and recharging requires a conscious effort to *notice* the sights, sounds, and smells intertwined externally and within us; the impact we have on self and others; the blessing(s) bestowed upon us while engaging in an activity. Notice attitude, emotions, and posturing. One of my coaching clients, who also happens to be an awesome minister, likened being in the moment to a breath prayer—the time it takes to say a short prayer in the span of a cleansing and focusing breath. Call it blessings, if you will.

Being in the moment clearly places us in the heart of the activity, connects our purpose, values and goals, and calls forth emotions and feelings that impart continuous motivating fulfillment. This moment is the only moment. When we fail to be present to it, we lose it forever.

Taking time to notice and be fully present in this moment in time lets us feel just how good life is, right now. It's not about reflecting or imagining the future. It's about breathing the moment inward, wrapping our senses around it, and embracing and hugging life to its fullest. It is total awareness, total presence. It can last an hour or a minute or the time it takes to inhale a long, lung-filling oxygenating breath. Take it, own it, and "be" in life while busily "doing" life.

A discharged, unplugged woman too often quits on herself. She goes through the motions of the day disconnected.

Dreams fade, her dignity and self esteem fizzle, and she "just exists." She's in deep "do-do."

In stark contrast, the Recharged Woman shows up! Her internal and external presence is alive in the moment. She combines "do" with "be" and successfully resonates "Do-Be-Do-Be-Do." While surrounding herself in "do," she fills her day with "be."

Imagine the possibility of cultivating a moment of solitude amidst the chaos and confusion of a full calendar. While standing in a bank queue or grocery line, reflect silently. It's your time if you choose it to be. Use each of the senses (touch, hear, see, smell, and taste) to stay in the present moment. Get a tape recorder, jot a quick note, or allot twenty minutes to meditate, take a walk, or sit. Do-Be-Do-Be-Do at a stop sign, in line, waiting at a youth sports practice, or trying on shoes.

I had an hour to spare before a presentation. It was an overcast, but fresh-air day—even in the heart of downtown Minneapolis. I really dislike the central city in general. You're always stepping in someone else's gum or inhaling the fumes from a passing bus. It's very noisy, irritatingly so.

I just wasn't ready to succumb to being indoors for most of this beautiful day, so I pledged to make the most of my hour. With the chimes of the historic jail clock clanging overhead, I discovered a fountain of dancing water and parked my fanny (bum, to my friends in Australia) on a nearby ledge. Noise was everywhere—

police whistles directed traffic, bulldozers tore up more streets, trucks backed up into delivery spots, cars honked from every direction, high heeled shoes clicked loudly alongside me, and even an emergency vehicle with siren blaring whizzed past my perch at the fountain.

Confusion and interruptions tested my patience. Yet, I dreaded going inside a windowless building on such a beautiful day. Challenged by my decision, I chose to be as present as possible, to "be in the moment."

As I gazed at the passers-by, I began to notice their cadence. The rhythmic sounds suddenly soothed my soul. Before I knew it, the fountain mesmerized me. I noticed my shoulders relaxing, my heartbeat slowing. I smiled. And, I no longer seemed to notice the grating sounds of the city. Five minutes of purposeful attentiveness to my surroundings brought about unusual, yet timely peace. My mind was free to enjoy that very morning and suddenly the day was exceptional.

The Recharged Woman is a Do-Be-Do-Be-Do Woman. She knows how to "be" in life while busily "doing" life. Even women whose lives have been changed by life altering events such as cancer can "be" while in the midst of urgency to "do more." What I know to be true for me is that anywhere, any time I can tune into more of me if only for five minutes or long enough for a cleansing breath. It's like taking a sneaker nap with eyes wide open. It's refreshing, engaging, and "being" fully alive in life. "Being" is Recharging.

Exercise—Sneaker Nap

Here's how you, too, can take a sneaker nap.

1. Stop—stand still, sit down, or lean against something.
2. Observe your surroundings—focus on one thing.
3. Now look at, and listen to that single focus—fountain, flag blowing, etc.
4. Focus while consciously relaxing your breathing.
5. Allow your body to relax.
6. Communicate with the object—which doesn't mean you need to really talk to it. Notice its movement, color, smell, etc. Imagine around it; be curious about the object.
7. Stay with it a while.
8. Begin to return to your schedule and notice a shift in attitude and demeanor.

Where do you choose to Recharge In the Moment?

Exercise—In the Moment

Set your watch, cell phone, or instant message reminder (task list) on your computer to engage several times a day. When notified, just stop for the moment and become fully aware and present "in the moment."

Ask yourself these questions:

- Right now, in this moment in time, what do I hear, see, smell, taste, and feel?

- How am I living on purpose and with full intention?
- What one thing do I choose to appreciate in this breath in time?
- What am I missing in my daily activities that keep me from satisfaction, fulfillment, and recharging my life?
- What impact am I having on the world this moment?
- What impact is the world having on me?

The Recharged *Woman*

- The Recharged Woman is a "Do-Be-Do-Be-Do" Woman. She knows how to "be" in life while busily "doing" life.

- The Recharged Woman shows up! Her internal and external presence is alive in the moment.

- The Recharged Woman connects the full spectrum of sights, sounds, smells, and tastes as a means of recharging in the moment.

- The Recharged Woman realizes this moment is the only moment to seize fully.

Connecting With *Contentment*

In college, those immature years when I thought I knew it all, my college classmates, professors, and mentors reminded me, "never be content." "Keep striving," they chirped. Having arrived at the ripe old age of twenty-three and knowing it all, I tried in earnest to live up to their philosophy. I even adopted other statements that chimed loudly in my ears—"The grass is greener on the other side of the fence" and "I want what I don't have."

> *It is not our circumstances that create our discontentment or contentment. It is us.*
> —Vivian Greene

Every day life pulled me outside of myself to carry out my work, perform tasks, meet objectives, measure results, and exceed expectations. Whether I was pounding on the glass ceiling or trudging through to-do lists, the outside world tugged at me for more—faster, with fewer resources—and it must be completed yesterday. Never enough.

While striving to have more (of the material world) and be more (of the perfect person), the message I perceived was: it will all pan out "in the future." But, the pursuit of happiness never came—and I found myself wallowing in unhappiness and discontent awaiting some future promise of pleasure. "What is this *thing* called 'contentment'?" I incessantly asked. The more education I achieved, the more financial security I accrued, and the more material possessions I accumulated, the less settled I felt. I swear the words "anxiety-ridden and hopelessly searching" were tattooed on my forehead. I was clearly a discharged woman, with barely enough spark to light my own life's fire.

Many of my clients overcame dysfunctional childhoods and horrific life events. I grew up in a stable, functional, seemingly normal environment. Yet, regardless of our differing pasts, we shared a common bond: to anxiously chase this thing called contentment.

Looking to the future for a distant promise of something better drained any ability I possessed to nourish my soul with the pleasures, gifts, and blessings right in front of my nose. My purpose for life and my values lost clarity. I was racing toward the future and forgetting that today is a precious commodity in everyone's life.

Then it hit me square in the jaw. Several years ago while sitting alongside a quiet bend on the Gallatin River in Montana, watching my husband fly fish, I noticed myself swaying back and forth to the rhythm of his fly rod effortlessly moving through the air, then nipping at the surface of the water. I noticed the water spilling over the rocks and felt my breathing slow down. My constant adrenalin rush and wild, darting, anxiety-prone thoughts of do-more and have-more began disappearing into a unique calmness. Mesmerized, I started to feel contentment. Oh my gosh, it was not a *thing*, it was a *feeling*! And contentment felt so-o-o wonderful. The problem was, I didn't know how to put this feeling into words, and today I still struggle to verbalize it. Here's my best effort. I hope it gels for you because it's one of life's awesome recharging gifts.

Contentment is the okay-ness, the peace a Recharged Woman generates within, in spite of the circumstances in which she lives. Contentment is honest self-acceptance without ego stroking. It is not about giving up. It is about aliveness in her plans and goals and achievements. It is about living consciously with purpose, awareness, and intention—and being content and secure with what *is* at this moment in time. Enough—right now.

Finding contentment doesn't mean stopping in time. It means recognizing the here and now, the present—how we feel, what we notice, who we are being in the balance of self, family and friends, work, faith, and play. Change, a daily occurrence in our chaotic world, often surprises even the most stoic woman, sometimes leaving her feeling vulnerable. Being content in the moment creates the space the Recharged Woman needs to be fully aware and capable of finding an internal peace around *what is.*

During my afternoon visit to the Gallatin River there were no phones, no contact with business associates, friends, or family. The paperwork and daily activities were visibly absent. I wasn't trying to seize the future that had not yet arrived. I wasn't searching for that promised pleasure. In this vast open space God created for me, I began to notice a whole different way of being. My hearing triggered a deeper listening. I listened to the water lazily lap the banks of the river. The deep river waters struck the imbedded rocks generating a smattering of rapids and a cacophony of sounds. Muscles relaxed and temperament calmed, my mind stopped screaming anxiously, and I noticed all the beauty around me—and within me. I felt my bony behind cradled between two boulders on the shoreline. The breeze whispered in my ear and softly twisted my hair. I was in the moment, *and* something else, too—content! I felt connected, grounded, grateful, and accepting of where I've been, where I'm going, and who and what I am now. Contentment for me was very forgiving and judgment free, not relentless and persecuting like the "anxiety-ridden" tattoo I was wearing on my forehead.

The more I enjoyed this feeling of contentment, the more I wondered if I could stay recharged upon my return to the real world. It's a funny thing about fate. While working with Carlie, one of my clients, contentment grew to be the topic of our coaching. Carlie's rendition of contentment goes something like this.

"My house is too small, I have no space to be creative. Stuff, there's stuff all over. It's either kids, their friends, my husband, or the pets needing attention. We're planning to move someday and then it will be fine. Maybe then I can have a garden and trees and room. It's so stressful. Life's just darn nasty. Someday it will be okay."

Carlie went to work discovering contentment. "My house is small. I bought containers and packed away the stuff we don't use regularly. Boy, did that ever create space. I made a small space in our bedroom where I can curl up in a chair and read a book. I have a wonderful lavender candle and a new lamp that takes up no space at all. I close the door. This is my space. I like it a lot. I feel good here. Even though I have a small yard I bought a few planters and planted the most beautiful flowers for my home (notice it's no longer a house). When the weather is pleasant, we all consciously spend more time outside. Home seems bigger and the inside seems less constricting. You know, it's really a pretty special home. Our kids have grown up here and we're right on the beach of the Pacific Ocean. Everyday we create new memories, and right now I'm grateful for what I have. I still keep a scrapbook of what I want in the future home, and I've finally come to look forward to the future while accepting now. The dread of living here has dissipated. Actually, my attitude is better about the whole situation. It's funny how the whole family seems a little more at ease too."

It is imperative that we look at what we have, not at what we don't have. We need to appreciate where we are in life. We can be rich without having a dime, if we utilize contentment in our life.

> *"...I have learned to be content whatever the circumstances. I know what it is to be in need, and I know what it is to have plenty. I have learned the secret of being content in any and every situation, whether well fed or hungry, whether living in plenty or in want."*
>
> —Philippians 4:11-12 NIV

Exercise—Contentment

Asking the following questions helps define and strengthen our own contentment in the here and now as we continue to set goals and attain change in our forward growth.

- What one attitude, thought, feeling, or action do I choose to take today to be more accepting of myself?
- On a scale of one to ten (ten being the highest), how content am I overall?
- What one conscious effort do I choose to make today to ground myself in contentment and increase my level of satisfaction?
- How does this effort impact me?
- How does it impact my surroundings?
- Who loses when I live only for the future or try to fix the past?

- Who am I when I accept myself and my place in this unique life journey I am creating?
- How does it feel to know I am enough?
- How does it feel to know that whatever I have right now is enough?
- How does it feel to know that what I am doing right now is enough?

The Recharged Woman

- The Recharged Woman embraces contentment as a way to find inner peace in what is.
- The Recharged Woman is self-accepting.
- The Recharged Woman makes plans and sets goals for the future. At the same time, she is grateful for where she is right now on the continuum of life.

Energy ℬoosters

Mirror, mirror on the wall, who's the fairest one of all? Not me, that's for sure! Redheads don't have all the fun. In fact, this redhead wore boxing gloves to protect herself from her inner *self*. I wasn't the prettiest girl in school, nor was I the tallest, lankiest, or most popular. I guess you could say I was run of the mill (and for me that was a stretch of the teenage imagination). Maybe it was the ribbing I received about my freckles or strawberry blonde hair color that crushed my spirit. "Red" and "Rusty" were nicknames echoed by classmates. Before Harry Potter made my maiden name famous, others subjected me to Potts, Rusty Pot, and Pothead. (No, I wasn't a Viet Nam era pot smoker). God knows there were days (and weeks and months and years) that I felt

> *It's the courageous and Recharged Woman who stands in front of the mirror and proclaims she is the fairest one of all— and believes it.*
>
> —Valorie Potter

intimidated by my peers' daunting comments. Was I overly sensitive? Maybe, but in those pubescent years my insecurities got the best of me anyway.

Over time, I developed a cleverly defensive shell, attempting academic perfection as a way to cover up my infrequent internal bouts of self-doubt. Parents, grandparents, and close friends repeatedly reminded me of my gifts and talents. Some days I felt accepting of myself—some days.

The subconscious mind works in images. Do you remember a time when you told yourself not to order French fries, but you vividly saw yourself enjoying every luscious bite? Then, without another thought, you surrendered to that powerful image. Likewise, negative images painted by insecurities are powerfully discharging.

Fast-forwarding through life, I matured into adulthood and seemed to survive with much more self-confidence and worth. The good days were really good. But, as is the case with many women, I still harbored very subtle, yet wounding and self-sabotaging thoughts about myself. Don't most of us carry similar baggage? It seemed easier to believe the icky thoughts than the positive ones. The problem was, I failed to ask one simple question, "What good does it serve me to smolder in self-sabotaging thoughts when I can live ignited in the inner truths about me?"

One brisk, but sunny February afternoon, deep in the heart of conversation with my mom, she pulled from her medicine cabinet a yellowed, well-worn clipping from an unknown periodical. It spoke many "I Am" truths, "I *am* the best person I can be today. I love who I *am*, even when others doubt me. I *am* deserving of love. I *am* deserving of internal peace and joy. I *am* God's gift and I shall use it to the best of my abilities. I *am* distinctively skilled. I *am* unique, special, and one of a kind, not to be compared to others."

My mom, one of the most positive and upbeat women I know, utilized a reminder list to reaffirm her worth on earth. Go figure! It was a revelation to learn that even upbeat kindred encounter downbeat periods of time. We all need a little help in life. I'm in awe of my mom's ability to recharge not only herself, but to recharge me using affirmations.

The briskness of that February day warmed into a huge energy shift for me—call it a light bulb moment. My mother had utilized various approaches to affirming my sister and me through the years. Her approaches worked a lot of the time. Yet, something was still missing. Why didn't I get it? More importantly, what was I going to do about it now? Wounded by infrequent, undermining lapses in self-esteem, my positive self-image suffered. Unaware, I engaged in self-defeating negative thoughts at various times in life. "I'm unattractive, I am unlikable, I am boring." That was a vivid picture. I repeated that statement so often that I actually believed it to be factual. It's true; we are who we believe ourselves to be. My subconscious mind was a huge inferno, and yes, I was fueling it. Yuk.

Finally, after years of ignoring my mother's success strategies for life, I listened to my mom from a totally different perspective. Turning the tables, Mom and I created a self-affirming list of truths about me. Was I ready to believe these truths? Hah! There was an emotional lifting, but I still needed a jolt of electricity running through my veins. "It's the courageous and Recharged Woman," Mom said, "who stands in front of the mirror and proclaims she is the fairest one of all—and believes it."

It *is* true. We are all gifts. Every day we choose our attitude. Every day we choose to engage in negative self-talk or affirm our worth with positive self-talk. Positive affirmations powerfully energize self-confidence. They are the "I Am's," that ignite our worth. They support our personal values. They require courage and a positive attitude to commit to long-lasting constructive change. Affirmations require a willingness to be vulnerable to our inner truths. Affirmations slowly unravel the crossed wires like guilt, fear, and anger—the barriers that impede our circuits from recharging.

Affirming one's self is a simple process, yet one that may feel very awkward in the beginning. Society suggests that when we toot our own horn, we are arrogant, self-centered, and conceited. Maybe that is the case in selected social settings. Stemming from our values, what we are about to power up are the inner truths about us, whether anyone else acknowledges them or not.

When we believe in our worth, we begin to trust our potential and our abilities. Acknowledgments are convictions. The first few times we practice affirming ourselves, we'll probably think it is a *s-t-r-e-t-c-h* to believe what we are saying. Press on, awesome woman. We're actually creating a new habit, a life-changing opportunity to feel really good about ourselves. (Remember, new habits take about twenty-eight consecutive days to lock in permanent change.)

Imagine the fun of the daily mirror challenge. Stand in front of the mirror. Look into your own eyes. Say something awesome to your self. Try saying it with a frown, with a grin, standing on your head. Whisper it, yell it, or proclaim it with all the theatrics you can muster. Over time, the truths you speak become believable.

Did you know that showing confidence on the outside scares away the fear on the inside? This is especially true when we succeed at quelling fear (which is what happens most of the time). Even though the inside light of confidence is awfully dim, to the rest of the world we can externally create the look of self-confidence—and over time, we become who we believe we are. After all, we are worth it. The Recharged Woman deserves to be self-confident.

While affirmations build self worth and confidence, they also build resiliency. We are continually bombarded by the opinions and judgments of others. As a recharged, confident woman, it becomes easier to brush off the tendency to live under the blanket of guilt and to buy into what other people want us to be like. We learn that it is *our* set of values and *our* inner strengths that drive us to happiness and fulfillment. When we know who we are, and we live from that place, we leave behind the stresses that others try to impose upon us. We create our own inner peace.

Exercise—I Am...

Ready? With pencil and paper, make a list of truths about yourself. It may take a while to come up with your list. Keep it growing. Own it, look at it, say it, declare it, and believe it. Remember, we are what we believe.

I am.....

I am.....

I am.....

Be careful to limit the words "I can" and "I want." These phrases put you in a dream stage, a "wanna-be" stage, instead of the here and now. This list comprises the bottom line personal truths. By the way, if your list is short, ask those you trust to notice who you "be" and write down one or two "I Am" affirmation statements they know to be true about you. My partial list is in the back of the book. After you have completed the exercise, feel free to peek at it.

Don't wait for your own self-confidence to appear. Big mistake. A *dis*charged woman waits for the confidence to build, and usually waits, and waits, and waits.

Affirmations are a powerful, forward-propelling step to increased confidence building even though the changes appear subtle at first. When I affirm who I am, I take responsibility for myself. I create the person I want to be, the person I choose to be. I am secure in my self-truths. You will be too.

Ask yourself:

- What will it take for me to stand in my own vulnerability and declare my positive truths and attributes?
- What do I choose to believe about myself?
- Who am I?
- Who do I choose to let others see?

The Recharged *Woman*

- The Recharged Woman believes that which she affirms.
- The Recharged Woman knows her truths are worth affirming.
- The Recharged Woman knows affirmations are the keys to unlocking the door to belief.
- The Recharged Woman chooses a positive attitude and commits to affirming her magnificence each day with statements that begin with "I am."
- The Recharged Woman is resilient to the opinions and judgments of others.
- The Recharged Woman is authentic and vulnerable to her inner truths.
- The Recharged Woman is a gift to herself and to others.
- The Recharged Woman is courageous.
- The Recharged Woman stands in front of the mirror and proclaims she is the fairest one of all—and believes it.

Shine the Light on *Listening*

"Uh-huh, uh-huh," my friend, Maddie, mumbled. I imagined her head nodding in agreement over my comments. I assumed this best friend and business associate was as heavily invested in the importance of this telephone conversation as I. In the background, I heard Maddie clicking away on her computer. She thought I could not hear her fingers flying across the keyboard. She obviously assumed typing and conversing at the same time was okay. My friend, Maddie, even satisfied my immediate need for conversation by pretending to listen to me.

> A *good listener is*
> *not only popular every-*
> *where, but after a while he*
> *gets to know something.*
> —Wilson Mizner

"Uh-huh, uh-huh," she repeated. Occasionally she threw in a frivolous question or a trite comment like "I get it."

Maddie heard me, but she really didn't listen to me. She finally announced that she was in the middle of a crunch time deadline. Why didn't she tell me this tidy bit of information before I started sharing my conversation with her?

Clearly my expectations for the outcome of the phone conversation were completely different than Maddie's. Clearly we both were assuming the other person was okay with the tone and direction of the conversation. We were both wrong.

Sh-h-h-h. Listen. Did you know that over half of our communication time is spent listening, and the only thing we do more of is breathe? Sh-h-h-h. Listen. Do you hear noises? Sure you do, because hearing is involuntary. The sounds go in through the ear canal and bounce around waiting for interpretation.

The ability to hear, however, does not equate with the gift we give to others and ourselves through *listening*. Listening is a purposeful event, one we engage in consciously. It requires tweaking not only our listening skills, but also our ability to trust and deem ourselves capable of interpreting more than mere words.

When plagued by the hustle and bustle of everyday life, we tend *not* to listen to what the *other person* is really saying. We miss the visual cues; we miss the unspoken language hidden between the lines of dialogue. We zone out. How many times have our children and co-workers talked to us while our thoughts were someplace else? We nodded, perhaps looked at the other person, but never really listened. We merely provided lip service and perhaps a smile or nod.

Whether alone or in conversation with others, the Recharged Woman is uniquely aware of two sizzling hot wires that short circuit her ability to listen—assumptions and expectations. Listening inwardly, she notices when she is electrically discharging by assuming.

Assumptions are the act of taking something for granted, presuming. Assumptions are our perception of the truth as we see it. Assuming is not necessarily backed up with proof. Unwanted and unnecessary tension arises within us when we *assume* the other person knows our thoughts, wishes, desires, and needs. We go on to assume the other person will act or react in a certain way. Unfortunately, we fail to take into account that we cannot control what the other person is thinking, or how he or she is feeling or behaving. When we assume, we risk miscommunication. We fail to listen at a deeper level for the clues of assumption making. In the earlier story about Maddie, I assumed she was willing to engage in an intimate and engaging conversation with me at that particular moment. As it turned out, she was not really connecting to my conversation in a way that I needed, and I became disgruntled. I felt let down and disengaged. Incorrect assumptions, therefore, create an aggravating short circuit.

The Recharged Woman avoids jumping into assumptions based on incomplete information. When in doubt, she asks clarifying questions to separate fact from emotion. She deliberately rephrases and restates what the other person says. It is essential that both parties gain similar understanding of the spoken word and its nonverbal signals.

Securing details eliminates any thought to compose static like, unrealistic, and discharging assumptions.

- Where do I notice I'm making assumptions?
- How does it affect me?
- What facts do I need to secure?

Expectations, which are beliefs in our mind that something will happen, leave us in a place of anticipation. In Maddie's story, I assumed she had time to talk. Further, I expected her to behave a certain way. I expected Maddie to sit still, put her computer aside, completely focus on my every word, and give me the feedback I needed. She, on the other hand, expected me to sense her frantic tone of voice and know her busy schedule, allow her to accomplish another task while conversing, and understand where her mind was prioritizing. Neither of us was listening for the non-verbal signals. Neither of us communicated verbally what our expectations were for the conversation. Both of us missed the mark.

Whether alone or with others, the Recharged Woman listens for her own expectations of self and others. She asks:

- Is my expectation for myself realistic?
- Is my expectation for the other person realistic?
- Have we clearly communicated the same expectation?
- Do the expectations of both the Recharged Woman and the other person synchronize so that the final outcome for both parties is very clear?

Listening is an incredibly important communication skill for recharging. Connecting at the deeper level of listening (versus hearing) requires the shift of focus from "me" ("what's in this for me?" and "what does this mean to me?") to "you" listening.

"You" listening moves a thought from self to what the other person needs us to know, verbally and non-verbally. Focus on the other person is more amped up and intense. Negative energy interrupters (sensory distractions) move into the background. "You" listeners plug into the conversation at a deeper direct current connecting level. The verbal and non-verbal cues of direct current connecting include eye contact, posture and physical gestures, voice intonation, and the presence and commitment to the other person to be fully present in the conversation.

Intuition plays an important part in the "you" direct current listening. Tapping into gut-level intuitive knowledge, the Recharged Woman reads between the lines. She gets into the heart and soul of the other person and connects into that person's internal pulse. When the feeling, the hunch, the magnetic message is stronger than the apparent logical combination of words, intuition is present. She listens inwardly to the little voice inside. She has déjà vu experiences, physical shivers, and vibrations. She knows what's "in the air" and answers the question "can you feel it?" She trusts her intuition.

As we continue to trust our intuition, confidence builds. Our intuition sparks curious questions, deepening the conversation and making it more personal and meaningful for both individuals engaged in this unique and precious dialogue. Common phrases that open our intuition to the conversation include "I have a sense…" and "My gut tells me….". Try them.

Overwhelmed and discharged women are often quoted as saying "I feel that I'm not being listened to, not being heard." Most people have poor listening skills. Implementing our listening tools assures us of being a better listener. While we cannot control the listening habits of others, we can create a better listening environment by our own actions. And when we choose to listen, our self-esteem increases; we trust ourselves and we build trusting relationships with others. Others are drawn to us like magnets. We are attractive and others seek to connect with us. Communication at its most intimate level occurs. We recharge.

- Where do I trust my intuition?
- Where do I notice my intuition calling me?
- Where do I choose to use my intuition?
- How does it serve my listening skills?
- How does it impact the other person?
- What one thing will I do today to impact my ability to listen differently in a manner that recharges me?
- Where do I notice the impact on my life?

The Recharged $\mathscr{Woman}$

- The Recharged Woman is a conscious inward listener.

- The Recharged Woman seeks details and avoids jumping to conclusions through assumptions.

- The Recharged Woman listens for, and interprets, realistic versus unrealistic expectations.

- The Recharged Woman's connective listening skill shifts the emphasis of listening from "me" to "you."

- The Recharged Woman plugs in to both the verbal and non-verbal cues of direct current "you" listening.

- The Recharged Woman trusts intuitive direct current "you" listening.

Establish Relationships that Energize Your Life

Where better to test relationship building than in the ski and golf resort of Big Sky, Montana? The locals hail their part of the country as the Last Best Place. Each day the 11,166-foot Lone Mountain peak greets this beautiful mountain village. Rugged and sometimes windswept, the peak balances its unforgettable rocky view with soothing blue skies, dancing white clouds, and the glistening snows of winter. In spring and summer, emerald green trees and grassy meadows complement the peak's ruggedness. In the autumn, the fluttering of red, gold, and burnt orange leaves softens the scenery. The view lures

> *One can never consent to creep when one feels an impulse to soar.*
>
> —Helen Keller

visitors into an intimate, somewhat sacred connecting relationship with nature. Businesswomen, moms, and grandmoms alike seek to work and play on the mountain. The whole atmosphere imparts in them the same great feeling they strive to share with guests—the feeling of connection.

What secrets does Big Sky hold? First, it embraces guests with a warm and gracious welcome. Everyone accepts you for who you are with no pretenses. No one seems to be competing with one another. There's no "keeping up with the Jones's" attitude. No one is judged on skiing competency, wardrobe, or income level. Resort guests and staff exhibit a healthy self-image. It's easy to begin to trust the interactions with others.

Second, when greeted, everyone genuinely wants to know how you are feeling. Maybe it's the majestic blue sky and crisp clean air that cleanses the mind and the ears because people really listen. On the mountainside and in the chalets, staff listen to the laughter and chatter of visitors. If something's not quite right, the folks at Big Sky work hard to create a positive lasting impression of friendliness and helpfulness.

Third, in fun (and to send a subtle message), there are "No Whining" signs posted about the resort village. The simple message: relationships rely on communications. Need help? Ask. Have an issue? Communicate to resolve.

Fourth, whether riding up a high speed chair lift or purchasing a frothy, steaming cup of cappuccino, someone always takes the first step to converse. That enthusiasm for personal connection is infectious. Because everyone is so friendly, it becomes immediately apparent to everyone when you are negatively discharged and disconnected. Big Sky is a great place to check your own willingness to engage in short term feel-good conversations as well as those that evolve into longer lasting relationships.

Fifth, staff freely praise and compliment one another. They compliment guests as well. On the mountain, it's common to witness vacationers and staff alike praising one another's style of skiing, rosy cheeks, or hearty laugh. Lift line attendants always cheer you on, finding something pleasant to share in the brief encounters of loading bodies into a gondola.

Sixth, Big Sky maintains a full-time guest relations department. The goal of the department's staff is to impart good will, build lasting connections with guests, and be a liaison between workforce and visitors. Further, staff make a concerted effort to improve themselves by way of input from all concerns. They do it by inviting open dialogue on the mountain, at the ticket window, in the restaurant, on the terrace.

No man is an island—and neither is a woman. Like Big Sky, the Recharged Woman thrives on establishing and maintaining meaningful relationships. Conversely, a short-circuited, overwhelmed, energy-drained woman throttles down into survival mode. She continually multi-tasks in an effort to fit into her schedule all of the demands that her professional and personal lives place upon her. Discharged, she loses contact with the very relationships that nurture her. She fails to develop new relationships in the wake of her busy schedule. With no feedback, her feelings of acceptance and self-worth diminish. How lonely and isolating is this existence? What kind of a life has she carved out for herself? Busy, perhaps, but sadly unfulfilled.

Relationships, whether with acquaintances, friends, or loved ones are essential to our well being. Mayo Clinic's HealthQuest newsletter reports that a strong social network is an important component of overall health.

Yet, when we are overwhelmed with too many commitments, one of the first things we give up is our relationship time with others. We limit our conversations and our face-to-face gatherings, even though such connections are the ones that unconditionally spark our full range of emotions from sorrow to joy, from anger to elation.

Author Stephen Covey in his book, *The 7 Habits of Highly Effective People*, writes about our Emotional Bank Account (a metaphor describing the amount of trust that's built up in a relationship). The account provides individuals with a way to calculate how their relationships either make deposits or withdrawals from that emotional account. Honest, courteous, caring, or kind associations reap the rewards of emotional deposits. Trust and safety, the core of intimate relationships, multiply many times over. However, when that trust and safety are depleted through disrespect, betrayal, or any kind of threat, not only are there withdrawals from the emotional bank account, but the chance of emotional bankruptcy heightens. We are social creatures, albeit defined uniquely by the number of relationships each of us needs. Words, expression, and touch fulfill and nurture our need to connect on a deeper personal level. Most importantly, the generation of emotional and recharging deposits must outweigh disconnecting and depleting withdrawals.

Void of the trust that builds our positive emotional reserves, we walk on eggshells, and look over our shoulder at our every comment or movement. We feel threatened, tension mounts, and we begin to self-destruct. Our energy level is displaced to the battlegrounds of barely tolerant and most often ineffective nattering.

On the other hand, a strong support system that develops deeper personal bonds breeds security, safety, integrity, and trust. It increases a person's identity, worth, and self esteem. Vested friendships flourish without strings. This priceless bond grants permission to express the full realm of ideas and emotions, share similar values, freely believe in a Higher Power, and share a vision each can respect and admire of the other. It demonstrates an interdependence rather than dependence in many areas of each other's life. Trusted friendships make it easier to seek and receive help. A trusted friend learns to forgive. The friendship thrives in the present not in the past. The relationship takes turns providing leadership for each other, supports the positive in each person, and does not enable the other to mire in negativity. Both sides accept and appreciate change, yet display a consistent behavior that sparks trust. Great relationships grant permission to ask for what each person needs without the other judging right or wrong. Strong, healthy relationships appreciate each other's uniqueness and cheer each other to greater potential especially during times of risk-taking.

We all deserve kindness, love, and acceptance in our life. We deserve to be trusted and to feel trusted. We deserve to feel safe in the very relationships that open the door to sharing our ideas and inner expressions. We deserve leisure time—time to breathe, relax, and share through laughter and tears without judgment. We deserve to be accepted without advice or criticism. It's a place to accept others' faults and imperfections as we strengthen our ability to accept our own shortcomings.

Exercise—Friends

Relationships come in myriad shapes and sizes. Husbands, high school buddies, and college roommates become "best friends." Distance in miles is irrelevant. Nurturing these relationships creates deposits into our emotional bank account.

Make a list of your friends and "best friend(s)."

Ask yourself:

- What makes each relationship unique and compelling?
- How am I choosing to nurture each relationship?

- What one thing can I do to further enrich and recharge that special association?

Other relationships bear the title "acquaintances." These might include greeting the butcher or checkout person with a smile that builds a relationship in that moment. Stopping to help a child or a senior also makes deposits into the emotional bank account.

Ask yourself:

- In the moment of the day, how am I choosing to increase my emotional bank account through expanding my acquaintances?
- What do I notice happening to me? To others?

The Recharged Woman removes herself from relationships that are toxic. She looks for the unhealthy discharging feelings of low-energy, boredom, emptiness, and indifference. Other toxic burnouts include relationships that breed lack of courtesy, trust, sincerity, and a positive attitude toward self and others.

Ask yourself:

- What one relationship do I recognize to be toxic?
- What tough choice am I willing to make in order to eliminate toxicity and recharge?

The Recharged Woman

- The Recharged Woman seeks to develop a variety of relationships that support her values and purpose.
- The Recharged Woman seeks to nurture her friendships.
- The Recharged Woman builds relationships wherever she goes.
- The Recharged Woman maintains a realistic self-image and doesn't compete with others.
- The Recharged Woman is aware of how others perceive her.
- The Recharged Woman takes the first step to converse. She does not wait for others to engage in conversation.
- The Recharged Woman gives authentic praise and compliments freely.
- The Recharged Woman takes time to invest in relationships that build deposits in her Emotional Bank Account.

Current *Questions*

"Who me? Ask for something? You've got to be kidding! Neediness is a weakness. I'd rather do it myself. That way it will get done right, within my time frame. Besides no one else can do it as well as me. And, if they could do a decent job, I don't have time anyway to teach them how to do it properly. You know, you can never trust others. What if they said 'no'? I'd just want to die of embarrassment for having asked. And, on the off chance that they said 'yes,' I'd hate to feel like I needed to pay the other person back. I don't want that problem of obligation hanging over my head!"

> *Ask and it will be given to you; seek and you will find; knock and the door will be opened to you.*
> —Matthew 7:7 NIV

Whoa! Whether we are moms, executives, line workers, spouses, friends, sales agents, or caregivers, we all have needs. Yet asking for what we need is often one of the biggest hurdles to overcome. Requesting help is not always easy or comfortable, especially if we have been taught from an early age not to ask. Like the example above, we have been conditioned to believe we should go it alone. We know, however, that we really do need help in life. In vowing to get over the "I can do it by myself" syndrome, consider the following perspectives on plugging in to asking for, and receiving, help.

Reframe negative, discharging thought patterns. Realize that neediness is not a weakness. Period. We live in an ever-changing world of technology. Even the best leaders have made a paradigm shift over the last few decades. They don't know it all anymore either, nor can they go it alone. Asking for help is a healthy responsibility.

Don't assume someone doesn't want to help. Often times, another person, even a stranger, wants to help. They just don't know the right words to use as a gesture of genuine offering. They, too, may be fearful of our rejection of "no thanks." The learning goes both ways. Asking for help creates goodwill. Risk it. What have we got to lose?

When we ask for help, understand that the other person might say "no." So what? Will either of us die on the spot? The answer is no. If the attitude is right, neither of us will feel bad. Much like sales people who understand that it takes a certain number of nos to get one yes, we can adopt a similar attitude. If one person we ask says no, go on to ask another person. We will get a welcoming yes before too long. It's in the numbers.

What about our concern for feeling obligated? Friends and loved ones usually don't place paybacks as a condition for helping. If they do place a condition upon the request for help, we have the power and choice to say no. We also have the ability to reframe the no. For instance, if someone asks us in return to run errands for them, we can say, "No, I am not comfortable doing that. Is there anything else I might be able to do to help you at another time?" This phrase clearly sets our boundaries, and at the same time speaks the message that we are willing to help them in the future, as long as it fits within our comfort zone. This technique is a form of negotiating, a pleasant verbal tennis match.

When we ask for help, try to choose a person who we believe will do a suitable job for us. Just as we wouldn't ask a girlfriend to lift a refrigerator for us, we also wouldn't ask an 85-year-old man teetering in a walker to tote three large boxes to UPS.

Asking for help sometimes takes on a different look, one of delegation. Particularly within families, delegating teaches responsibility, sets community and personal boundaries and expectations, and affirms family values. When used wisely and without intentional abuse (the "I'm lazy, you do it all routine"), everyone wins. Self-confidence and respect for self and others increases in everyone.

When we receive help, it is critical to adjust our attitude to appreciate the gesture. Accept the help with grace, dignity, and gratitude. How many times are we caught off guard by a simple offer of help? "No thank you," we say without even thinking. People offer for a reason—they want to help! We don't even have to ask. AND, we need to learn to receive it. The Recharged Woman toggles the energy switch to full power by saying "yes, thank you."

Accept also that the help we receive may not be perfect. However, the job is more complete than had we not accepted help. Enjoy the company, the gesture, and know that it is as good as it gets right now. The offer to help was generated in good faith and with a genuine desire to do a satisfactory job.

When faced with teaching someone how to carry out our request for help, it is always helpful to look at the big picture. Just like enthusiastic children who squeal with joy at the opportunity to learn to vacuum and dust and sweep and wash cars, everyone benefits from a little bit of nurturing and proper training. Spending a little time now to teach the other person how to help us means that in the future, we can ask the same person for help again, and feel more confident that the job will be completed in a satisfactory manner. Most people want to please one another. The attitude of "can do" and "isn't this fun" makes the job much more likely to be done with grace and accepted with gratitude.

> *Know how to ask.*
> *There is nothing more*
> *difficult for some people,*
> *nor for others, easier.*
> —Baltasar Gracian

We also need to accept that there might be tasks for which we cannot request help. We will either manage to complete the tasks or let them go. We are the ultimate boundary maker in our own lives.

Déjà vu. Last evening, I visited the weed-infested flower garden I ignored all spring. As I bent down, I heard my name being called. My energetic (and really fun) neighbor, Natalia, a young mom of three, jumped between her garden and mine. "Are you planting or pulling weeds?" she asked jokingly. Rolling my eyes back and giving a giggle, I replied, "Pulling so I can plant." "If I get my garden gloves, may I help you?" Natalia queried. Not thinking, I started to suggest she just look on and keep me company, but in that moment, I agreed to her offer.

Returning with one dirt-laden orphan glove (over which we laughed, then groaned viewing the prickly weeds abounding), Natalia reminded me how much she missed not seeing me this spring. As the evening wore on, we talked about missing each other, our husband's golf games, her young kids and my older one, and our families. We vented, chuckled, and mutually cursed each time we accidentally clutched a thorn. What a wonderful reunion. Natalia and I worked in a bit of exercise from bending at the waist, she got away from the kids for a while, we enjoyed our special friendship, and we discovered that we both enjoyed pulling weeds. It seemed to be a therapeutic exercise. While there were no conditions of payback from this receipt of services, we both decided that it might be fun to plant some new bushes around her deck. Providing it fit into my schedule, I also agreed that I would like to help her. Best of all, we discovered by accident, a new commonality. We strengthened our relationship because Natalia *wanted* to help and because I *chose to receive* help.

Ironically, if you believe the quote from Acts 20:35 that "It is better to give than to receive," then isn't it better to give someone who wants to help you the opportunity to help?

The responsibility of asking for help isn't just to receive physical assistance for a task we're unable to accomplish alone. It's so much more. Here are some other reasons to strengthen our asking muscles. Can you think of more reasons?

- Ask for the sake of understanding and clarification.
- Ask for the sake of reducing the fear of the process.
- Ask for the sake of curiosity.
- Ask for the sake of engaging in conversation.
- Ask for the sake of creating goodwill.
- Ask for the sake of reducing stress.
- Ask for the sake of building deeper personal relationships.
- Ask for the sake of being heard, being a part of a team.
- Ask for the sake of balancing your life.
- Ask for the sake of honoring your values.
- Ask for the sake of teaching others to ask.

- Ask for the sake of satisfying your needs.
- Ask for the sake of increasing your self-confidence.
- Ask for the sake of giving others the chance to help.
- Ask for the sake of helping someone else and reaping the personal rewards.
- Ask for the sake of conquering a new skill.
- Ask for the sake of supporting your goals.
- Ask for the sake of seeing whether you die when someone says "no."
- Ask for the sake of learning how many nos it takes to get a yes.
- Ask for the sake of practicing setting boundaries and negotiating possible paybacks.
- Ask for the sake of establishing a new relationship with someone else.
- Ask for the sake of giving yourself one more permission tool.
- Ask for the sake of practicing the art of receiving help with grace, dignity, and gratitude.
- Ask for the sake of recharging.

Here are more simple coaching questions to consider:

- What do I gain by going it alone?
- What do I sacrifice by walling myself off from help?
- What is the worst thing that can happen if I ask someone for help?
- Can I live with that possibility?

- How might my life change for the better if I receive help?
- How would that feel?
- How might others feel?
- How might my existing relationships change?
- What new relationships are waiting to be discovered?
- How will my stress be reduced?
- When will I see my life returning to more balance?
- Where will I see my life returning to more balance?
- What more in life is there for me when I ask?
- How much better can life be as a result of asking for, and receiving, help?
- What will I commit to asking for today?

The Recharged Woman

- The Recharged Woman understands she needs help.
- The Recharged Woman asks for help.
- The Recharged Woman knows what she is willing to offer in return for help received.
- The Recharged Woman chooses to accept help with grace, dignity, and gratitude.

Outrageously Extreme
Self Care

Threading this book is the theme of self-care. Sure, we know that eating right, sleeping well, and engaging in regular exercise are good for our physical, emotional, and mental health. But there's a walk on the wild side I invite all of us to take. It moves us from the take-it-for-granted and heard-that-information-before boring routine of good self-care to the exciting and slightly daring edge of Outrageously Extreme Self Care.

Self-care is not only good for us, it is essential. Various studies confirm that increased stress reduces our ability to fight off illness and disease. Our immunological systems become over stressed and resistance to disease is reduced dramatically over time. Self-care is such a basic need that we frequently take it for granted. Most of us endure losing a little sleep here and there. Our diet isn't always

> *Today is the day that counts most. Settle less often. Be outrageous!*
> —Pamela Nelson

the best it can be, and statistics show that we just don't exercise enough. Over time we develop numbness to what's good for us and grow too comfortable with that which is slowly making us sick.

The alarm clock no longer chirps a pleasant and inviting reminder of a new day. Instead, it haunts us with the cue that our chores are beginning again, relentlessly. We gulp down lots and lots of coffee to stay awake; we may smoke to take the edge off the tension; we drink adult beverages, just to unwind a bit; we snack on fast food and bags of chips.

Not only is our body worn down, but our spirit spirals right along. Too tired to vacuum? Too tired to sleep? Too tired to take a refreshing walk along a river's edge or next to a lake whose waters gently lap against the rocky shoreline with an almost mesmerizing and calming rhythmic tune?

Where are we willing to look at our attitude toward self-care? Where are we willing to step out of the mundane, dreary, unhappy, and unhealthy lifestyle and begin to take back the person that everyone loves and needs in their lives?

We have heard it a million times—"you have to take better care of yourself." Perhaps we did a good job of self-care before being thrust into a new life as a caregiver, new spouse, parent, or career woman. Are we sustaining that continuing commitment to health? Hooray, if we can proclaim so. Let's keep it up and celebrate our accomplishments. We deserve it.

However, if, like many of us, the daily grind has given way to poor self-care, now is the time to recharge. Permission granted. How does the word "extreme" resonate? Is it a little intense? Overpowering? Wake up! Self-care is about extremes. We are often extremely busy, extremely overwhelmed, extremely careful to meet everyone else's needs, extremely sensitive to criticism, extremely tired, extremely stressed, extremely out of balance. Therefore, extreme self-care becomes the single most important nourishment we can give to ourselves.

So what is outrageously extreme self-care? The *outrageous* is stepping out of the norm to create excitement, intrigue, challenge, and fun in all that we do with, for, and to self and others. It's the challenge to look at self-care as a necessity—then implementing it from a new and electrifying perspective.

Outrageously extreme self-care is defined by your personal desire to take personal care to a level of playfulness. Not all of the following ideas will appeal to you. That's okay. Life is about change, so try an idea or two that appears intriguing. Make up your own outrageous and healthy alternatives. Some of the following ideas include various ways to add humor, carve out time, and create solitude and resting of the mind: meditating, progressive muscle relaxation, T'ai Chi, yoga, sneaker naps, and reflection. Read on and open your mind to the possibilities.

Laugh and the world laughs with you. Stub your toe and the world laughs whether you do or not. From giggles to belly laughs, humor in our life recharges us. Our physical bodies are loaded with God-given miracles too technical to mention in detail. In generalities, we comprise pain-killing hormones called endorphins that kick into high gear when we laugh. Endorphins insulate us from a certain amount of physical pain. A generous belly laugh increases the production of T-cells, interferon, and immune proteins called globulins. These goodies strengthen our immune system and help ward off illness. Under stress, the harmful hormone cortisol increases. Giggles lower cortisol levels, returning our body to a relaxed state. Giggles even help us overcome certain fears by relaxing our tendency toward increased anxiety.

The gift of laughter changes our perspective on life. It allows us to take life a bit less seriously and triggers our naturally creative side. Children awaken to a fresh new day filled with an overabundance of creativity. Listen to children at play. They express amusement with the simplest of activities. Make a silly face, try to dance like them, or crack a joke and watch a child wail with uncontrollable laughter. Humor and creativity go hand in hand.

Some of my coaching clients' outrageous expressions of humor exhibited through playfulness and laughter include shopping and purchasing toys for themselves and bringing them to home and work. There are hundreds of toys from the Slinky to wind-up walking toys, from spiffy pencil toppers to the cheap goofy-eyes glasses. Run to the everything's-a-dollar type stores. Drive to the children's toy stores. Power walk to garage sales and flea markets. But first, you must change your mindset. You must consider this an important adventure into finding the very best (mostest funnest, cooler-than-coolest) giggle goody (or two or three or ten). Don't forget to play with the toys!

A perfect example of extending playfulness into our serious lives occurs every time I visit my dentist. Truthfully, I dislike going to the dentist's office, even though I'm very routine with my visits. To ease my anxiety, I brought a pair of silly eyeglasses to the visit one day. The staff loved the glasses. It changed the otherwise serious tone of the office to one of lightheartedness. Upon departure, I left behind the glasses. At every six-month visit, the staff dons the glasses. I giggle, relax, and enjoy my visit with much less anxiety. I am reminded of the continued pleasure those silly glasses bring to staff and patients. Stressful days are a little less stressed. Frightened children and adults humor themselves by looking into the mirror and parading around the office. Giggles abound. The cost? $1.00. The rewards? Countless.

Carve out time. It bears repeating, the more time we give to ourselves to re-energize, the more time we have available for others. We thrive on impacting communications and rich, meaningful relationships with God, self, and others. Whether we choose to carve out time in huge chunks or in little increments (waiting to heat a cup of coffee in the microwave, before anyone else gets up, in the bathroom, or right in the middle of the day), we *need* to be good to ourselves. The word *carve* implies a conscious effort to pen in non-negotiable self-care time. Many clients find the words *pen* and *non-negotiable* outrageously extreme challenges. How will I commit to challenging myself to carve out time for me?

Mirror truths talk. Notice the physical changes calling us to truth telling. Light up the full-length mirror. When exhausted, how many visual messages are ignored? Is our skin parched? Have our eyes lost their glimmer? Is our hair dull and a bit less stylish? Do we settle for less? Is the truth in the mirror a picture we avoid? Do headaches, heartburn, aches, and pains accompany us more frequently? Do the soft lines around our eyes appear deeper set than usual? Does a frown line appear more often on our forehead? Mirror, mirror, what's the truth I'm afraid to admit? What basic self-care have I ignored? What outrageously extreme self-care will I tell the mirror I'll change? What results will I see? What needs to change?

Cut the chatter. Rest the mind. Continuous background chatter elevates our stress level. We speak louder, we listen differently, and we often take in more useless information than our minds need to acquire. Constant chatter from the radio, television, noisy venues including restaurants, and work environments dull our critical listening skills. We replace listening with selective deafness. Too much chatter builds often-silent barriers to the closeness of certain relationships.

Resting the mind slows heart rate and breathing, decreases oxygen usage, lowers blood lactate, and reduces anxiety. Two components assist in achieving a quiet mind: the repetition of a sound, word, prayer, phrase or small body movement, *and* consciously eliminating competing thoughts and chatter that fight to enter the mind.

The outrageously extreme self-caring Recharged Woman uses, among other things, ear plugs, takes quiet retreats, walks alone in quiet locations, sits in quiet cars, listens to relaxation tapes, keeps a water fountain running in her room, uses white sound machines, rides a bike with the wind blowing in her ears, and floats in a warm, relaxing bathtub, ears gently immersed just below the surface of the water. Her relaxation techniques also include meditation.

To meditate, sit comfortably in a quiet place. Close your eyes, and consciously relax your muscles. Breathe through your nose and begin to reduce the breathing rate. Silently repeat a word, prayer, phrase, or sound every time you exhale. "Om" is a common mantra that has a calming vibration to it. Maintain the mantra. Notice when distracting thoughts enter the mind. Refocus. Spend ten to twenty minutes meditating if possible. Meditate in small increments of three to seven minutes throughout the day. When complete, sit quietly alert for a few minutes. Enjoy.

Where do I notice background chatter in my life? What action steps do I take to reduce the background chatter in my life? What affect do I notice from resting my mind?

Our bodies deserve a break. Where do you notice your body tensing up? Is it in the shoulders, neck, head, or scalp? Do you clench your fists or jaw? Many books offer relaxation exercises. If you don't already have a few exercises in mind, take time to discover what works for you.

Progressive muscle relaxation, an easy and effective practice, starts by lying down in a quiet location, arms at your side. Tighten head and neck muscles, and then relax them. Keeping them relaxed, move to the facial muscles. Tighten, and then relax. Continue with the shoulders, arms, hands, and so on until the toes are tensed and relaxed. Lie still for ten to twenty minutes. With repeat practice, your muscles will learn to relax and stay relaxed.

T'ai Chi, an ancient Chinese art, consists of graceful, slow muscle movement combined with conscious mind and breathing techniques. T'ai Chi promotes the free flow of energies (chi) and leads to a recharged state of being.

Yoga provides stretching and body posturing with controlled breathing. It energizes the Recharged Woman while relaxing her body. Basic stretching also rests the body and reduces tight muscles.

I always enjoy closing my eyes, when possible, taking a very deep, cleansing breath. I inhale slowly. I imagine clear, clean oxygen entering my body, filtering life into me. I slowly exhale the cloudy, polluted air that has exhausted my body. I repeat this exercise three times. At the same time I notice my body relaxing. Ah-h-h. It brings peace to my being.

Stepping into the outrageous, I'm famous for taking sneaker naps, and I don't apologize to anyone. Before I snooze, I tell myself to awaken in twenty minutes. Like clockwork, I bring my body to a relaxed state within the twenty minutes, awaken, and resume my daily activities. And, no, I'm not the kind of person who can fall asleep on a whim. My body tells me it needs a nap. I then attempt to oblige my body's messages. Even if I cannot snooze for twenty minutes, I have at least ceased movement and relaxed for that amount of time.

Have you read a good book lately? One of my clients in California has two very active children. Her children build playhouses and tents with tables and blankets. One day, after a coaching session, Mom, too, discovered the joy of tenting. For one hour she chose to be still. She rested her body by reading and relaxing inside the tent her children erected for her. During that hour in her "playhouse," she discovered a world of outrageous solitude. She listened to herself. She listened to the environment.

What do you do to honor your body's signals for rest? Where is there a pleasant place in your home, work environment or community to rest? What will it take for you to test it out? What's the reward for having rested?

Reflect. Different than resting and clearing the mind, quiet reflection allows us to savor the magnificence that we bring to ourselves and to the rest of those whom we influence. Time for reflection is time to acknowledge our magnificence. It's internal glow time. It is time to be in a state of appreciation for self and what we bring to this world. We know what we know, and we recognize it. Reflection is not a time to reflect on the negative, although it can be a time to identify the positive next steps after a challenging situation has occurred. While affirmations build the muscles of confidence and higher self-esteem, reflections appreciate the work that affirmations bring to our "knowing" self.

Every day I use my computer. Outrageously reminded to reflect, I post breathtaking photos of places that have impact on my life. Every time I open my computer, I am compelled to reflect, if only for a moment.

Answering the following question(s) creates space to reflect.

I feel good about myself because _____. I appreciate the wonderful person I am. Others appreciate me because _____. I lift my performance level by _____. My life balance is improved because _____. When I contribute to others I contribute to myself. I contribute by _____. I feel courageous when _____. I feel peaceful when _____. What awesome, outrageous reflection builds internal strength and peace?

Journal. A very effective way to keep your reflections close at hand is to journal. Those of us who keep a journal understand the impact it has on our lives. For those of us who have yet to discover journaling, just begin writing. No rules, just write. Pen and paper provide space to vent and solve problems through left-brain analytic perspective combined with right-brained creativity and intuition. Journaling is a historical tool to track trends and life changing events. What if you don't like to write? I personally use a pocket tape recorder. It's with me nearly all of the time. When I choose not to pen my words, I speak my reflections. Journaling clarifies feelings and thoughts. We will get to know ourselves better.

Nighty-night time. We know that quality sleep is imperative to our health. Yet, how many of us are disciplined about getting the appropriate amount of sleep? I'm guilty, too. What I do know is that every time I get a decent night's sleep, I feel recharged. I'm a more pleasant and patient person, my nerves are steady, my attitude is positive, and I love being a part of the day.

Are you a television junkie? Is it difficult to turn off the tube in order to get a decent night's sleep? Is it difficult to let go of the day's activities? Coaching clients suggest the following extreme ideas: tape the television show and watch it tomorrow; use the answering machine to take messages after 8 P.M.; create rituals that end the day peacefully, including prayer; make the bedroom a comfort zone; no paperwork allowed, especially no book editing! No TV unless it really helps you to fall asleep.

Then use an automatic timer to disconnect the power. Tune into only pleasant, non-stimulating programming.

My outrageous sleepy time gift is a small water fountain and a timer. Each night it starts up before my husband and I retire to our room. It greets us with instant calm, and it shuts itself off about a half hour after we fall asleep. I also tuck a small CD player and speakers into the nightstands. We shed our stressors listening to methodical melodies. On a scale of one to ten, ten being the highest, how do you value quality, healing sleep? What are you doing to keep it a priority in your life? How do you choose to engage a better sleep pattern?

Creativity. We all have it. It just needs to be unleashed. Creativity occurs when old ideas are combined in new ways. Outrageously extreme self-care requires creativity and an attitude of "can do."

Get a massage • *paint your toe nails* **• tickle your toes with a pedicure •** *beautify your face with a makeover* **• schedule a fake bake (sunless tan) •** *star gaze* **• moon watch tromp through the tall grass •** *go on a picnic* **• slide •** *swing and teeter totter* **• get your finger nails dirty •** *get a manicure* **• make snow angels •** *rent a hilarious movie or a chick flick* **• share it with a friend •** *spit sunflower seeds* **• skip rocks along the water •** *use paper plates, cups, and plastic silverware* **• pet a dog or cat •** *shed the* *eat popcorn* *inhibitions* • hug a child • *engage in mad, passionate love-making* • get naked • *cry loudly* • laugh relentlessly • *and shout in celebration* • dance • *sing* • jump on a trampoline • *jump on a bed* • build a sandcastle • *light a fire or candle and focus on the flame* • imagine your future • *engage in safe stress!* *climb a tree* • wildly tempt yourself to say "no" five or six times a day where you would normally say "yes" • *be face painted* • break the morning coffee routine • *drink water* • sip on a frothy mocha frosty shake • *feel naughty* • imagine the possibilities • *find joy in life's small wonders* • stretch when nobody's looking • *stretch when everybody's looking* • look right back at them • *really, really listen to sounds* • smell fragrances • *feel the sun's warmth* • turn around • *notice what's there* • feel yourself being held tightly, securely • *repeat the phrase "I love me"* • share the words "I love you" • *make someone's day and make yours as well* • sleep outdoors • *bungee jump* • eat sushi or a new food you have never dared to try • *walk farther than you have ever walked* • walk in

doodle

sing out of tune

sleep late

suck on a Popsicle

a straight line and have someone pick you up at your destination • *hum and feel the vibration in the back of your throat* • stare at the flames of a controlled fire •

listen to your heart beat

hire someone to do something for you • delegate • *delegate some more* • stop reading the newspaper • *give up coupon cutting* • have your children take you to the park and let them make the lunch • *enjoy the love that went into the effort a child makes* • drink water colored and flavored with fresh fruit, mix it with cranberry juice • *pray* • give your kidneys a break, go potty often • *have your children design a very special do not disturb sign that they get to hang on the door when you take a very long bath* • use the sign often • *breathe slowly and with purpose* • listen to music that relaxes you • *affirm yourself daily* • place a mirror on your desk and smile at you throughout the day • *hang a visible sign that reads "I am magnificent"* • hang another sign that reads "I am deserving" •

close your eyes often

skip lunch and get caught up on phone calls

buy yourself fresh flowers

believe both signs • forgive • *prioritize lunch over other obligations* • spend your valuable time with other people who are uplifting and sup-portive • *dump the nay sayers, the nasty negatives in life* • visit a farmer's market and taste every-thing you can • *bring home something fresh to share with your family* • include family in your activities • *exclude family members from your activities* • close your eyes at work for five minutes • *wear earplugs* • learn to golf, speak another language, or _____ (you fill in the blank) • *create boundaries* • take a nap • *get reacquainted with someone you haven't seen for a while* • take a vacation—if only for an hour or a day; look forward to it with all the excitement you can muster; your vacation might be sleeping in, or having someone make you breakfast or taking care of the elder for a day or slipping away for a retreat with your spouse • *volunteer if it feels right* • stop volunteering when it's a burden • *practice saying "no" with authority and gentle-ness* • stop apologizing for things that don't

ask for what you need

be sneaky (but honest)

give up guilt

install caller I.D. and use it

really need an apology (yes, it is respectful and serves a purpose. When we apologize because we feel "less than" or "not good enough," we dig ourselves into a hole of worthlessness. If we were worthless, we wouldn't be the magnificent person we are.) • *take in a movie* • release your emotions • *have a party* • finger paint • *make root beer floats and slurp through the straw* • giggle • *blow bubbles* • divert, detour, veg out • *quit your job, or negotiate some flexibility* • find the blessing in the moment • *be a curious four-year-old and ask questions* • take photos or digital pictures • *capture new memories* • begin your legacy to the world • *make no excuses* • engage optimism • *work out differently* • look at your tongue in the mirror and feel it • *ride a roller coaster* • ignore the doorbell • *share a dream* • belly laugh for practice • *belly dance* • learn to perform an illusion • *invent something* • create a new habit • *explore the night with a flashlight* • tell the truth faster • *buy a pair of shoes that actually fit* • dare to leave the house without makeup • *embrace intimacy* • share a thunderstorm or fireworks display with a friend • *be spontaneous* • nourish yourself like never before • *accept and celebrate you.*

dump pessimism

drool

break an old habit

find passion

- How many other outrageously extreme self-care activities can you think of that will tickle you from your nose to your toes?
- What one thing do you dare to take on?

The Recharged *Woman*

- The Recharged Woman engages in creative and outrageously extreme self-care.
- The Recharged Woman deliberately carves out the time she needs to feel whole and complete.
- The Recharged Woman promotes quiet time to rest the mind.
- The Recharged Woman savors spontaneity as her ignition switch to fun and freedom.
- The Recharged Woman retreats into reflection. She gets in touch with her inner greatness and finds gratefulness in all that she is.
- The Recharged Woman savors and honors proper sleep.
- The Recharged Woman embraces laughter and humor in her life.

Grounded in $\mathcal{G}od$

He doesn't charge overtime rates; the phone line is never busy. He never puts us on terminal hold, and He doesn't require us to set an appointment with Him three months out. His planner always has a spot open with our name on it. We never have to repeat our name, nor do we have to spell it again and again. His voice is the voice of trust, truth, hope, freedom, love, joy, and faith. He is easy to talk to. He listens and is fully aware. He is all-knowing 24/7/365.

> *When you want it, ask for it; believe in it, listen for it, then you'll receive it.*
> —Pamela Nelson

What I've learned is that we all need to be grounded in a power or spirit greater than us. For sake of argument, let's call this Higher Power, God. God is our faith and our hope. We may not have the same spiritual beliefs, and that's okay. We're not talking about religion of rituals, sacred rules, and sacred buildings. We're talking about God and achieving an intimate relationship with this Higher Power. The Recharged Woman develops and nurtures this unique and intimate relationship never to be compared to that of others.

I didn't always know these traits of God. My journey with God began as a wide-eyed impressionable youngster. I attended church in my ruffled petticoats and pretty pastel dresses. I even remember wearing hats and dainty white gloves. I partook in religious education, prayed at mealtime and bedtime. God's impact on my life, however, was not all encompassing. I relied on my mommy and daddy to know all and to keep me safe and secure.

As I grew older and seemingly wiser, Mom and Dad still answered my questions, helped me determine my course in life, set the rules, taught values and morals and the principles of living with God at my side. As I matured into my teen (know-it-all attitude) years, I noticed my parents weren't the end-all of information. They couldn't fix everything, nor could they answer some of the really curious and complicated questions about why Grandma got sick and died. I still loved and respected my parents and kept asking the questions anyway. I still needed them in my life on a daily basis even as I began to rely more on God to answer those really tough questions and guide me through life. God's impact in my life was slowly becoming more visible.

The first step toward success is taken when you refuse to be a captive of the environment in which you first find yourself.
—Mark Caine

Oh sure, I bumped in and out of practicing my faith in God as I experienced highs and lows in my life. I was too busy (or so I thought—remember, I knew it all as a teen) to consciously commit to God in my life all the time.

But, and here's the big "but," I kept sensing an uneasiness, personal compromise, a lack of contentment, and a void. Moving from home to college severed the "parental unit" ties even more. College was the real deal, noisy, chaotic, fast-paced, enticing, shocking, risky, fun, really fun, and really different. Maybe it was the homesick feeling that resurfaced every week or so, or maybe God was just knocking on the door a bit louder that prompted change. Either way, I opened the door cautiously, and His presence provided new comfort to me. I started noticing a sense of calm come over me whenever I invited God into my life. Prayer connected me to the Recharging Light that seemed to have flickered on and off in the past.

Okay, I still didn't quite "get it." There were occasional signs of bargaining with God. "Dear God, please fix it." "Dear God, if you _____, I'll never again do _____." At least when I bargained with the Big Guy in the Sky, there was a foundational belief that God was listening and answering my prayers.

It was more than the "biggies" (confirmation, marriage, nearly dying, son nearly dying, close call in the car, cancer scare, and a dozen more huge life events) in life that drew my attention to God. Once I started noticing the little stuff, the daily blessings right in front of my nose, then I realized the depth of the relationship God was showing me. Too many coincidences lit up the sky. I couldn't ignore His constant presence.

I admitted honestly that God had control. I started to let go of my urge to control every event, thought, action, and feeling in my life. He guided me into a recharged mode in times of need and times of celebration. He recharged me with courage and undying strength to face my problems and overcome adversity. His wisdom and guidance rendered my fears and guilt powerless. He switched my perspective from "I have to fix it" to "He can handle all my problems." He taught me to "let go" (a typical empty nester syndrome). Knowing He had a plan for me lifted from my shoulders the overburdening weight of my problems. I learned that my plan of action wasn't necessarily within His time frame. It didn't matter that others judged me. It didn't matter that others didn't accept me. God accepted me.

Life is sacred and it has been given to us as a gift. We become what we believe. Paraphrasing Paul in Phillippians 4:8, he invites us to think on those things that build us up, not those that tear us down. We should keep doing the things that are pure, pleasing, honorable, and right since the God of peace will be with us.

Bottom line: We can achieve relative success and balance in our lives over and above where we are today. But, to really ground it, God needs to be at the core of our lives (see the Conduits of Life Balance Wheel in Chapter

Five). God is the Higher Power at the center of our contentment, fulfillment, and peace. Find God. Invite God into your life. Trust God. Listen for God. Listen to God. Believe. With God at the center of your life, all things are possible.

- What one thing will I do to bring God into the focus of my life?
- How much better can it get with God in my life?

The Recharged *Woman*

- The Recharged Woman believes in the divine presence of a Higher Power called God.
- The Recharged Woman actively seeks the peace God provides.
- The Recharged Woman is grounded in God's love.
- The Recharged Woman develops and nurtures a unique and personally intimate relationship with God.
- The Recharged Woman knows that balancing life is dependent upon God being at the hub of life's activities.

Get a *Coach*

Coaching clients are amazed at the improvement in quality of life after implementing even a single idea from this book. I trust you, too, have become more aware of the power of the Recharged Woman. What greatness lies ahead for you! The possibilities abound for a Recharged Life.

Like so many of our past attempts to change, however, we often get bogged down. We begin to recharge and the short-circuiting crossed wires of anger, guilt, fear, and the like appear again. These dischargers creep

> *I've been absolutely terrified every moment of my life and I've never let it keep me from doing a single thing I wanted to do.*
> —Georgia O'Keefe

back into our head and before we know it, there is a whole cheering section ready to defeat our good intentions and our purpose. They scream in our ear, manipulating our every effort to change.

Change requires commitment. It also involves the sustainable actions that bring about the Recharged Woman's choice to create lasting meaningful change. This requires nonjudgmental support and continued accountability to see her through until change flows as a recharged part of life.

Well-meaning, well-intentioned friends and relatives usually create an all-too-familiar comfort zone of permission to backslide into old ways. Perhaps the term "enabler" is appropriate. These emotionally linked friends and relatives spare the edge walking (risk taking) it takes to build the courage to move forward. Enabling comments include: "Oh, it's all right." "You don't need to do that now." "Don't put yourself through this..." "We love you just the way you are."

Enablers usually live from a place of fear—their own fear. They are afraid to change, and they fear that the Recharged Woman might change too. Their fear is so huge (even though it is invisible to them) that they might be left behind—so they drag the Recharged Woman back into the same old place. The status quo is safe for them and they don't want the Recharged Woman to wander out of that status quo no matter how much it might be hurting her right now, let alone into the future. Well-meaning friends and relatives impose their insecurities on the Recharged Woman and attempt to suck her right down the musty, dark hole of fear right along with them.

Remember, change is a conscious choice we make. While it may (and usually does) serve/benefit others, ultimately our commitment to change is about our needs. When we choose to change—to recharge—life will be different. That may mean that those who choose to remain in a life of their own fear will have less of us. Decisions are not always an easy part of change, and it is a huge opportunity to let go of what isn't working in our life. It is also a wonderful way to model what others can choose to have also; they just haven't figured it out yet. So, hooray for the personal courage to commit to change.

If you cannot find someone to hold you accountable and support your decision to recharge, then I embrace a warm, sincere invitation to find an appropriate coach to hold you accountable for your discoveries, choices, and lasting changes. He/she is the catalyst who absolutely walks with you on your journey to finding your potential and becoming the Recharged Woman.

Beware, however. Anyone can hang a shingle above his or her door proclaiming to be a "coach." The gold standard for professional coaching is a certification from the International Coach Federation (ICF). This assures you that your coach has adhered to stringent educational and ethical guidelines and sustains a lengthy, proven, and continuous track record. ICF certified coaches have achieved either the Professional Certified Coach (PCC) or Master Certified Coach (MCC) designation. Minimally, Non-ICF certified coaches should carry a certification from an ICF approved coaching school.

When investing in an ICF certified coach, you can be confident that your coach will walk with you in your challenge to discover and change from a place of courage, honor, and integrity. Unlike therapy and counseling which answer a lot of "why" questions, focus on healing the past, and give advice, coaching is forward moving, future driven, and client-driven. A coach is an electrically charged conduit to recharging you. He or she is a partner in your agenda. A coach presumes you are functional and well. While you may have crossed wires that you alone have had difficulty pushing out of the way, your clear intention is to move forward in your life, to attain more balance, to live from your defined values, to seek happiness and fulfillment. An ICF certified coach positively impacts the Recharged Woman's ability to build a trusted coaching relationship in a judgment-free zone of strict confidentiality.

The Recharged *Woman*

- The Recharged Woman recognizes those enabling relationships that cause her to stall in her growth.
- The Recharged Woman trusts herself to know when she needs a coach.
- The Recharged Woman enlists an ICF certified coach when she is stuck in her forward movement toward personal fulfillment.
- The Recharged Woman accepts she is an active participant in her coaching experience.

Congratulations! You added a valuable toolkit for recharging. Keep lighting up your life in ways that honor the woman you choose to be. I am excited for you!

Let me know how I can support you —

Pam

Appendix

Partial Listing of
Values

Below is a partial list of values. Please don't use this list until you have exhausted your own list of values. If you can't think of at least ten values, then refer to this list. Be careful that you don't create a list of "wanna-be" values—values that you wish you were implementing and living.

Accomplishment	Collaborative
Accuracy	Competitiveness
Acknowledgment	Contribution
Adventure	Creativity
Authenticity	Directness
Autonomy	Elegance
Beauty	Empowerment
Career Fulfillment	Ethical
Certainty	Excellence
Challenge	Faith
Clarity	Family Closeness

Fear of Failure
Focus
Friends
Free Spirit
Freedom
Full Self Expression
Growth
Harmony
Health
Honesty
Humor
Imagination
Independence
Integrity
Intimacy
Joy
Justice
Lack of Pretense
Leadership
Love
Loyalty
Mastery
Moderation
Nature
Nurtured
Orderliness
Participation

Partnership
Peace
Performance
Personal Growth
Play
Power(ful)
Privacy
Productivity
Recognition
Resilient
Respect
Risk Taking
Romance
Security
Self (knowing)
Spirit
Spirituality
Success
Task Accomplishment
Tradition
Tranquility
Trust
Vitality
Well Being
Wellness
Wisdom
Zest

Partial List of **Affirmations**

I am a pleasant person.

I am able to let others see my faults.

I say NO.

I am lovable.

I am the best that I can be today.

I am responsible for my decisions.

I am able to self-correct when I am faced with a challenge.

I am interesting to some people, and not to others.

I am content knowing that I have lived from my place of excellence today.

I am not willing to bankrupt my emotional bank account with lame excuses.

I am filling my emotional bank account by practicing this exercise every day.

I am able to write creatively.

I am confident that my book will bring insights to readers.

I am committed to making this the best book I can for my reader.

I am confident that this is the best effort I give to the book and that nothing humanly created is perfect.

I am happy with that knowledge.

I am confident my book can help someone become the person they want to become.

I am confident my book can help a discharged woman become the Recharged Woman.

About the *Author*

Pamela L. Nelson, CPCC, PCC, is a success strategist and founding partner of the performance, improvement, training and coaching practices of Polish Your Potential and Nelson Success Group. She works with people to create their personal best and with organizations to generate and implement strategies to improve employee performance.

Pam is an internationally certified success/business coach, seminar leader of executive and managerial development programs, and adjunct faculty member at the University of St. Thomas and the Minnesota State Colleges and Universities (MnSCU).

She is principal in four successful businesses, three of which are international in scope, a member of National Speakers Association (NSA), International Coach Federation (ICF), Toastmasters International (TI), and American Society for Training & Development (ASTD).

Please direct your questions and comments to:

Pam Nelson
Nelson Success Group
702 40th Avenue NE
Minneapolis, MN   55421
651-330-1PYP (1797)

Pam@PolishYourPotential.com